A SHATTERED SOUL

My Life With
Dissociative Identity Disorder

Eve N. Adams

Acknowledgments

Iwould like to thank Dr. Tom Hawkins of Restoration in Christ Ministries for the groundbreaking work he has done over the last 30 years for the severely traumatized and abused to bring them to Jesus for healing and freedom. Without his commitment and work it is questionable whether I would have been able to get the results I, and many others, have gotten. He has trained people in all 50 states of the US and worldwide how to bring the traumatized to Jesus for healing. You can contact him through his website www.rcm-usa.org.

INTRODUCTION

This is my rendition of the way GOD chose to bring about my healing which may be different from the way God chooses to bring about your healing. I have written this book to give God the glory and I have portrayed my life in very graphic terms.

You could find yourself being triggered when reading this. I tell you this right now so that you are not surprised and can even pray to prepare yourself for the work that God will do in you by being triggered thru this real account of a Christian who has Dissociative Identity Disorder. God wastes absolutely nothing in His economy. So many times I did not understand this; I hope to spare you unnecessary suffering by convincing you to go along with the process despite the pain it causes you. God is big enough, powerful enough and loves you enough to bring you to healing no matter how big the resistance against it. To that I can testify over and over again.

If you are reading this and do not yet know Jesus, the information presented can still bring you healing because all truth comes from Jesus the healer. He will meet you where you are and is completely able to bring you to faith in Him. He wants to love you.

CONTENTS

IT WAS AN EMERGENCY

Hello, is anyone in there?
I said, HELLO!!!!!!!!!!! ANYONE???????????
No answer. I must have gone crazy or lost it. That was not the first time and it wouldn't be the last time I would ask that question. But because I then understood how my brain worked, I had a suspicion of what had gone on in there!

I had just had the strangest sensation, a "volcanic sensation" or perhaps a "volcanic feeling" might be a better way to describe what had happened. I had co-facilitated a Christian 12-Step Meeting with my husband one night at our church and there had been music playing from the boom box that one of the participants had brought for the first time. They had also brought snacks and the ingredients to make coffee, the rich smell of which had permeated the room. But even the heavenly smell of just-brewed JOE wafting over the aisles of chairs had not inhibited that "volcanic sensation" from having bombarded my consciousness and threatening to actually have me physically destroy the room we had been in. It would have been more accurate to say that the sensation wasn't a threat, but rather what my brain had wanted my body to do **with** that sensation that was a threat. I had learned that having feelings was neither good nor bad; it was what you did with them that was crucial. Sin occurred very quickly when I tried to handle strong emotions by either burying them inside myself or acting out. In my experience I had found that the best thing to do with strong emotions was to petition God to take them away so that I could remain in a Godly posture even though my insides raged.

"It" wanted me to pick up the maroon padded metal chairs one at a time and hurl them across the length of the 12 rows of chairs until they broke the glass which formed the entrance to the (storefront) building where we had our meetings. "Someone" in my brain had been "triggered" by the words that had been sung by the man on the CD which emanated from the boom box about 3 feet away from me. The man singing was praising Almighty God for His goodness. The exact words he sang are not burned into my memory or the name of the man or the title of the CD but that "volcanic sensation of rage" still remained.

I had immediately begun silently, and without indication on my face, **begging** Jesus to quell this reaction which was certainly not on MY agenda for that meeting. (Proverbs 29:11 – a fool gives full vent to his anger but, a wise man keeps himself under control). The topic of the meeting had been giving up control to God! I guess I had learned the lesson right then. (Romans 12:1–Therefore I urge you brothers in view of God's mercy to offer your bodies as living sacrifices holy and pleasing to God. This is your spiritual act of worship). It had become clear to me why God might have allowed this to have happened to me; He told me to tell the women in the group what had happened inside me during the worship time. The first question for the discussion that night had been about "pride". It sure had been pride, all right, to want to resist letting anyone know that this horrific reaction (in my opinion of the reaction) had happened and why; but I KNEW I had to "die to self" and be real about what had happened to me just minutes before. (Colossians 3:3, 9 – For you died and your life is now hidden with Christ in God....do not lie to each other) The volcanic sensation" had been triggered by the overwhelming rage that I had been feeling because I felt God had NOT been that wonderful to me like He had been to the man on the CD. No, in my mind God had been asleep on the job or not even aware of my plight for most of my life. In my mind, I had been such a bad child that God had let me get what I rightfully had coming to me. That sure reveals what my concept of God was like at times; despite over 30 years of learning that what I was told in my childhood **was truth** *was really lies, distortions and unholy, unrighteous authority* manipulating my vulnerable, innocent mind.

After the "sensation" subsided I thought; "Well, that was that". My life was over or at least the being facilitator of our group part of my life was over. The women in that evening's group had all been from the same residential recovery program and their leader, "BJ", had come with them to observe what the group had been doing. One of her group members, "CM" left the room searching for her after I had made my disclosure. "BJ" had been in another room in the back of the building with her fiancé and my husband; being briefed on the previous lessons, so that what we had been doing that night would make sense to them. I didn't find out until we had left for home after the meeting that "CM" had been highly upset and had been desperately insisting that "BJ" *had* to leave what she was doing *right then* and come back to the main meeting because *"it was an emergency!"* When "BJ" inquired of her what the emergency had been, she would not say; just that "BJ" had needed to come out front to the main meeting *immediately.*

Meanwhile, I had continued on to the next question in the lesson with the women who were left in the main meeting with me. I wasn't concerned that "CM" had left the room; the Ladies' room was also in the back of the building where she had gone. She could have gone there to use it. Not everything that happened was always all about me!!! Some of the remaining women said that they appreciated my honesty to allow them "in to me see:" (intimacy). They said that many people would not have disclosed what had happened as I did because it could be construed as my having had a sinful proclivity. Although I had been afraid I would be judged on how *good* a Christian I had been and would have been found lacking, I spoke up anyway. Would YOU want to have someone with that sinful proclivity being a facilitator of a group like I had been? I was supposed to have been the one who had it all together, having "arrived". I mean wasn't that what being a "leader" of a 12-Step Group had been all about? The women weren't leaders of the group because they were still struggling with addictions, one of which might be rage, so it logically follows that I ***shouldn't*** have been struggling with rage because I ***was*** the "leader". (1 Peter 3:4 – Your beauty should not come from outward adornment...instead, it should be that of your inner self, the unfading beauty of a gentle & quiet spirit, which is of great worth in God's sight).

Just the word leader was a misnomer because while I may have had more experience and/or recovery under my belt than others, only JESUS had been and is sinless and until we have left these bodies behind we will still be sinners. If that were not true, Jesus would not have had to die. We would have no need of Him to live Godly lives by the power of the Holy Spirit.

I realized I had also made the situation more difficult because when "BJ" interrupted my discussion with the women about the next question in the lesson, I told her that I felt that my reaction had had a demonic component. The demonic realm had been controversial in the Christian church at large then and in years past. I had not realized at that moment that perhaps the women's understanding of the demonic realm was not the same as mine. 12 Step Groups are secular which would have allowed for differing beliefs about many different religious concepts.

I had been sure "BJ" had wound up having to calm "CM" down and had to explain to her that there were differing beliefs on the demonic realm. I had assumed she had had the requisite knowledge. It was common in those days to state that one must deal with their demons, which was understood to have meant dealing with the mental/emotional issues that caused you to have acted in ways that were not effective to the life you had been trying to live. It had *not* referred to actual evil spirits!

My own understanding of the demonic realm had been developed over the last 40 years through much searching, instruction and experience; and based upon those concepts I believed that part of my "volcanic sensation" was, indeed, exacerbated by my demonization. You can see I said *demonization* not **demon possession.** There is a difference between the two and unfortunately the translators of most of the versions of the bible did not distinguish between the two. It was believed by most evangelical Christians that a Christian cannot be possessed by a demon because they are possessed (owned) by Jesus and the Holy Spirit lives in them. A Pre-Christian can indeed be *possessed by demons* and the demons can control their life. Demonization of Christians took place in the soul; i.e. the mind, will and emotions, but the Christian had control over the demons through the power of the Holy Spirit.

In one analogy, demonization of a person could be compared to a person having contracted a cold. The cold virus produced uncomfortable symptoms which had been there until the body rid itself of the virus which had been causing them. The body had not been *possessed* by the cold; the virus had been using the body's machinery to reproduce itself. If a person had taken care of themselves, the cold disappeared. With demons we also had to have taken care of ourselves so that they disappeared. A further discussion of my theories of the demonic will appear later on in this book.

'BJ" decided to have us put our chairs in a circle and she prayed for me and the women. By allowing her to have done this, my obedience to God had been tested. I had had a choice and I had chosen humility and treating others better than myself. (Phil 2:3b – but in humility consider others better than yourself; Romans 12:10b – Honor one another above yourself). When "BJ" had gotten finished praying, I asked one of the women to get the men so that we could have closed the meeting with the Serenity Prayer, but the women had not wanted to wait, so we had prayed and closed the meeting without the men. They had grabbed their stuff and had gone home.

None of those women had been back to another meeting. As a matter of fact, there had been no attendees the week after that. I had had a feeling of fear in the pit of my stomach and had been glad for the week off. I had been waiting for a disaster to happen because of how things had gone at the meeting described above, but there had been no phone calls, e-mails, text messages; nothing had notified me that I had been relieved of my position of having facilitated that 12-Step program. The following week we had been out of town and therefore there had been no meeting. When the next week had come there had been two new people. One of them had come up to me in church the Sunday before inquiring about our meeting and they had attended the week after we arrived back from being out of town. Praise God, I had thought; He still had believed in me and in my ability to have represented Him to the wounded and hurting!!!!

I had been so upset over what had happened at that initial meeting, that the next day I had called the professional counselor that I had been seeing, and asked if he could fit me in to discuss what had happened. I had not wanted to cause pain or problems for those who had come to the 12-Step Meeting; to have arrived expecting one thing and having wound up with something else. My husband and I had been very diligent to have followed the program guide-lines to the best of our understanding of them in our meetings and at that meeting I had been unable to maintain that commitment. If my continued need for healing had manifested itself during the meetings because I had been unaware that I could still have been accessed/ triggered, should I have continued to be a co-facilitator? My counselor told me that I had done well for myself and that God was going to continue to heal me and take care of those who attend those meetings; after all: Romans 8:28 – And we know that in all things God works for the good of those who love Him who have been called according to His purpose.

That Sunday in church, I felt that God rewarded me for my willingness to be a "living sacrifice" to those women. (Romans 12:1- Therefore I urge you brothers, in view of God's mercy, to offer your bodies as living sacrifices, holy, and pleasing to God, this is your spiritual act of worship) His presence was so strong during worship that day that I felt I needed to get down on my knees and face in awe of His glory. His presence remained strong during the sermon. The Pastor made an altar call for those who had doubt and even though I was *so* tired of going up every week in response to the altar call, I knew I had doubt and it was holding me back from what God had for me to do in His name, so I went up. The Pastor prayed for all those who came forward and then dismissed us back to our seats. Then the worship team played the final song. I stood up and raised my arms toward the heavens in praise and at that moment God "threw a ball of anointing" at me. His presence was so strong on me that I almost fell over backward, which would have had me bounce off the chairs; but instead I knelt down on my knees and put my face to the ground. Forget about what people think, I HAVE to obey God. (1 Sam. 15:22 – But Samuel replied, Does the Lord delight in burnt offerings and sacrifices as much as in obeying the voice of the Lord? To obey is better than sacrifice...) Needless to say, it was a very pleasant surprise to have God confirm His opinion of me in such a personal way. Praise Him. I had been pondering whether or not to resist the Holy Spirit when He was moving like that because this was a new church to me and I didn't know how the Pastor would feel about one of his congregants "resting in the Holy Spirit, second row center". But, God told me that I was being a people pleaser (Galatians 1:10 - Am I now trying to win approval of men, or of God? Or am I trying to please men? If I were still trying to please men, I would not be a servant of Christ). So I made up my mind to just let Him run things and I'll do what He wants, regardless of what others think.

I had occasion later in that week to speak briefly to the Pastor and he didn't even remember what I had done on that Sunday until he thought about it for a minute and then he said I was fine. I told him that I had one of the women come up to me after the service and ask if I was "all right". So I figured that not everyone in the congregation had had the teaching about or experience of the power of God falling on them and the Pastor said I was correct. Most of the congregants would wonder what was up if I were to "fall out" in the Spirit; thinking that perhaps I needed medical attention. My own father had that experience in a previous church of ours and he thought the man had had a heart attack because of his obvious age and convincing passed-out look. The man was fine and so was my father after we explained what had happened to that man!

Several weeks after that meeting, we had the state representative of the Christian 12 Step Program and his wife come to our church to give their testimony about the Program and afterward we ate lunch with them. It turns out that even with all the reading of the Leader's Manual and the kit that accompanies the Program that I had gotten some aspects of the nitty gritty operations of the program wrong. The type of meeting that I had been holding was a "step" meeting and that type of meeting should have been held on a separate night from the general meeting. So, at the next meeting, I ran the meeting in a completely different way, more in line with what the State Rep's had said they ran their meetings. The following week we had no attendees. I guess they didn't like the "new" format of the meeting. Since there had been no one there that night I took the opportunity to open the leader's guide again and noticed that after completion of the first three principles (steps), the group becomes closed to newcomers. Since there had been no attendees at this meeting it looked like the program would have to end. Now I understand why the people who attended this program in other locations and then came to ours thought that it was done some other way than what we were doing!! It was. I'm so glad that I can cry out for mercy to Jesus and He gives it to me.

The following week's meeting was nothing short of God Ordained and orchestrated. There were 21 men there. The men had been at the Sunday Service when the State Representatives were there, which at this point, was several weeks prior.

My oldest child volunteered to substitute last moment for my husband who did not attend that meeting and she did beautifully in helping me direct the meeting. I was so proud of her, she really helped me out. When we pulled up to the church there was no one standing there waiting for us and I didn't think there would be but I made a commitment to be there whether or not anyone else ever attends. A man came up to my car and asked me if I knew what time "that" meeting started. I told him 7 pm, and it was 7 pm, and I was going to open the church up and have a meeting. The men were so very appreciative to have a Christian 12 Step Program that they could attend because it was so much more difficult to go to the other 12 Step Meetings in our area where a "higher power" could be a desk drawer but you can't say JESUS is your Higher Power!!! Several of the men were touched by comments that were made during the meeting and they loved the teaching and workbook that I gave them to work in until the next meeting. I was so blessed to see several of the men just saved and just clean and they just bubbled all over the place about how great a God we serve. It gave me courage seeing and hearing their faith and they were so excited that they could come back and there would be coffee, snacks and worship. But, they didn't attend the next week, as a matter of fact; no one had attended since then.

Our Pastor was concerned that the men hadn't returned the next week and tried to contact the person he knew at their residential facility to find out what was going on. He never received an answer.

He made contact with "BJ", from that initial meeting where I was triggered and the women never returned to another meeting. He met with my husband and I about the program, at which time he informed us that "BJ" had left her position at the Residential facility (so the ladies had no ride) and moved out of our town (too far away to attend any of our meetings). The Program had several meetings a week in that town. This information showed me that God was using everything that happened for my good. I was getting healing that I didn't even know I needed, Praise God again.

GROWING UP IN A CULT?

The bible says that *before the creation God chose us* to be His own. (Ephesians 1:4a – For He chose us in Him *before the creation* of the world that we may be holy and blameless in His sight.) The Lord God formed man from the dust of the ground and breathed into his nostrils the breath of life…the man became a living being. The LORD God said, "It is not good for the man to be alone. I will make a helper suitable for him. Then the LORD God made a woman from the rib he had taken out of the man, and he brought her to the man." (Genesis 2:7, 18, 22). I read through the bible and I began learning about why I was created, and what my purpose was for being here on the earth. (Ephesians 1: 11-12 – In Him we were also chosen, having been predestined according to the plan of him who works out everything in conformity with the purpose of his will... God's intent for me was to be whole; and even at the time of my creation, God had a plan for my life, a plan to prosper me and not to harm me, plans to give me hope and a future (Jeremiah 29:11-12 – For

I know the plans I have for you declares the Lord, plans to prosper you and not to harm you, plans to give you a hope and a future.

I had been taught a system of beliefs that originated from both the Bible and religious tradition or ritual which word is better to describe the programming Cult members are given all through their lives. This form of religious control is one of the characteristics of a cult which I knew nothing about way back then; indeed, it was only when I began to get deliverance and inner healing that the characteristics of the cult began to manifest in me:

- Such as bowing the knee to anyone or anything other than the Lord Jesus Christ) i.e. bowing before any Monsignor, any Bishop, any Cardinal, and even the Pope. (1 Tim 2:5 - For there is one God and one mediator between God and men, the man Jesus Christ, who gave himself as a ransom for all men-the testimony given in its proper time)
- Such as another way to God other than Jesus Christ i.e. Mary the mother of Jesus, and the Saints. (John 14:6: Jesus answered, *I am* the way and the truth and the life. No one comes to the Father except through me.)
- Such as that there is any other solution for your sin other than the blood of Christ Jesus, i.e. the past practice of buying indulgences to "pay" a person's way out of purgatory, (1 Tim 2:5-6: For there is one God and one mediator between God and men, the man Jesus Christ,

who gave himself as a ransom for all men-the testimony given in its proper time).

- The praying of a novena (a long series of specific prayers) to get a person out of purgatory, which implies that Jesus' death wasn't enough to pay for all the sin a person would commit during his life; human effort (works done by humans' money or prayers) must be added.

- Such as that your eternal salvation is provided through any other way than the death, burial and resurrection of Christ (John 11:25: Jesus said to her, *I am* the resurrection and the life. He who believes in me will live, even though he dies) i.e. doing more good activities than bad activities.

- Such as that you add anything (any work of your own) to Christ's death; and offers you spiritual rules or regulations other than those God clearly teaches; i.e. classification of some sins as mortal, requiring more penance than others; others classified as venial, requiring less penance to pay for them. Also the classification of the catechism of rules based on the traditions of the Universal Church as equal to God's Revealed and Inerrant Word, The Bible to grant salvation from one's sins.

- Such as depending on any philosophy or activity that refers to accessing or relying on forces, spirits, powers, energies, etc. other than the Holy Spirit or anything that offers you spiritual enlightenment apart from God's Word.

- Finally, such as insisting on absolute loyalty to the group. (Condensed from Eddie Smith's book, "Making Sense of Spiritual Warfare").

Both the Bible and tradition were held in equal esteem and importance in the church I was born into, with that denomination's hold on my family going back to the early 1900's in countries outside the US before my grandparents had immigrated to America. The countries that my ancestors hailed from were very much ruled by the church; let's just say there was NO DIVISION of church and state in any matter. The Church WAS the state and its representatives had a supposedly direct ancestral bloodline back to when Jesus first founded the Christian Church in the geographic area that is now recognized as the Middle East. The church had absolute power over its members because they were BORN into the faith, they had no choice about what they did or didn't believe. Their parents knew they were Christians because *they* were Christians and *their ancestors before them were Christians* as far back as had been recorded.

That control facilitated corruption through the government officials whose beliefs and behavior were ruled with the iron fist of Rome, the center of The Church where its Supreme Leader, The Pope, was in residence. In order to have this kind of control over the people, the people needed to know exactly how they were expected to behave. This was accomplished with education. The fact that I had never read any of the Bible myself until I was 21 years old and had left the church complicated matters. In those days, the congregants were not educated by reading the bible, they read the catechism and the priests told them what *they* felt they needed to know, only.

Since I was born into The Church it would follow that my education was very thorough and efficient, carefully outlining from **Kindergarten** exactly what motives, omissions, attitudes, and actions were sin and how I was guilty of committing all of them. The Parish Priests alternated visiting the classrooms of the attached grade school at least once a week and to a 5-year old they looked like giants. Some looked like bears!!!! So I already knew about **Hell** where the bad children went, at a very early age, and I had a terrible fear of going there. Each day we would be drilled on our catechism regarding the rules of the church, the commandments, and the seriousness of sin; resulting in punishments of differing severity for committing said sins. Confessions on Saturday afternoon scared the tar out of me; I always thought that the Priest inside knew exactly who I was and what sins I was hiding so I wouldn't have to say more Hail Mary's or Our Fathers. (The Priest DID know who I was, there weren't that many little girls coming to confession EVERY Saturday). Confessions exemplified the concept of the sermon: "Sinners in the Hands of an Angry God" that the Reverend Jonathan Edwards preached in the 1600's.

By 3rd grade I already knew about purgatory, which was the place your soul went to burn until the payment for sins you had forgotten to confess before you died would be made. That scared me most of all because I knew I couldn't possibly remember to confess every sin when I committed it and some things I did I didn't even know were sin so how was I to confess them in time? I had plenty of help from the educators in the school both lay and religious about when I was being bad and was even told that God could see and hear everything I say or do when I think *I am hiding my sin* by physically hiding my body or hiding inside my mind all these sinful thoughts. They didn't have to be there to see me sin and punish me, GOD HIMSELF was watching me all the time and HE would be sure I got my accrued time in purgatory if I was lucky enough to do more good than bad before I died; if not I would just go directly to HELL forever. All of these rules and traditions and schoolwork took a lot of time to learn perfectly (we had to recite them every day and memorize them).

I spent many days in the Principal's office for my misbehavior. It wasn't even willful disobedience sometimes, but now I know I had ADHD (Attention Deficit Hyperactivity Disorder) and my brain wasn't neurologically matured enough to act in the way that was expected of me. My mom was so frustrated by me that she took me to the "General Practitioner" doctor who took care of our family and asked him for tranquilizers for me. He denied her request and gave them to her to take. I believe it was then that the "wait until your father comes home" punishments began. My grades were not good in the early elementary years; I barely passed and thought I was stupid. It turns out that between the undiagnosed and untreated ADHD, and the emotional insecurity and instability at home, that I couldn't learn. I couldn't remember what was taught, which caused fear, which exacerbated the inability to remember and on and on. I grew up being told that the truth was that "something is WRONG with me". Not like other kids who *did* wrong, no, I AM WRONG!! All you had to do was look around and you could see that something was WRONG with me. I clearly did not have what it took to be "right". Until recently I hadn't connected the specific time period to the threats of being sent to the "bad girls' home" because ***I was too BAD,*** indeed I was ***irreparably BAD***. I suspect this threatening was during these early elementary years because I was too young to understand that they would not be allowed to get rid of me to some "girls' home"; they had no intention of actually doing it, they just used it as one more attempt to get me to improve my behavior, i.e. be an adult at age 5.

FAMILY LIFE

I truly have no memories of my family life until shortly before April of 1959 when my little sister was born. I had been told by one of the neighbors across the side street from my house that they found me asleep in their driveway with my pillow one morning after my sister arrived. I was four when she was born and the neighbor girl, "FB", who lived there was a few months older than me. I don't remember how I knew her at age 4 but we did go all the way through to 12th grade in the same schools and in an extra-curricular activity as well as through High School. Like me, she lived in a one parent home; her father abandoned her and her 3 brothers when she was quite young. With her being the oldest, she carried a lot of responsibility too early in her young life as well. Maybe that's why we wound up friends of sorts. We shared a similar misery that we couldn't completely understand. She was one of the few girls that I ever allowed to come into my house and then for brief times to "play dolls or something". I remember being inside her house once in a while as well. "FB" and I did go to Girl Scouts together for a period of time but I had to quit because the leader had pierced ears and that was the sin of mutilating one's body. I could not be under the leadership of a woman who so flagrantly disregarded the Church's rules. I guess you could say "FB" and I were friends who drifted in and out of contact with each other over the last 50 years (more in than out). When she turned up pregnant with no means of support I told her the name of the doctor who did my abortion and he had become her regular "female" doctor for the last 30 years or more, while I moved away and found a new doctor.

My mom was non-functional for most of my life; my father and an assortment of other people did the cooking, cleaning, childcare, etc. Her diagnosis was Catatonic Schizophrenia, but at 5 years old all I knew was that mommy was sick. So mommy appeared and disappeared without much information for a number of years. Aside from the psychiatric diagnoses she had several physical difficulties that required operations and recovery at home. I have several seconds-long flashes of her being "sick" physically and I was left with the impression that it hurts to be sick and that my mommy might not get better. If I were sick enough I might disappear too. I guess that observation helped create the idea that my being sick wasn't good either. I was a bother, especially when the doctor who took care of us came to the house to check me out and I would run away so that he couldn't give me the shot I always received. I remember my mom being home alone with me then because I couldn't pull that stunt if anyone else was home. The doctor knew how sick my mom was so he was very patient with me for her sake. His daughter was a student in the same school I went to, he and his family were very good Italian church adherents.

But what was interesting was that when I was sick I was allowed to stay in bed and watch TV. Someone would bring me soup or something to eat in those early years. In the older years I did it myself. I got to be someone other than the "bad girl" that went to school and caused trouble; and I got to become someone else. I might have felt awful physically, but I got some kind of emotional consideration. Don't think that that meant I enjoyed crying myself to sleep because my ears hurt so badly many a night. The continuous ear problems might have been because of an undiagnosed milk allergy. I was told later in life that I was a horrible baby until they found the right formula, so it would make sense that my earaches were caused by the same thing. All three of my children had allergies and ear infections/fluid in the ear, etc. but we've had minor problems with my grandchildren's ears so far.

I was sick so much in first grade that I was supposed to be retained but the sister teaching my class was so caring that she worked out a way to get me through to the second grade during the summer. This sister was one of the few at the school who were gentle and loving. Because of her, I went to the school during the summertime to help the sisters prepare the classrooms for fall and even got to go inside the convent and see what it was all about. I recall I wanted to be a sister and devote my life to

God at an early age. Some of you might be thinking at this point that that was just a reaction to the crumbs of caring that I received from the sisters and which I thought were so wonderful at that young age; but I know that even though all of what I was being taught about God wasn't accurate, God gave me a deep desire for Him, a love for Him despite the confusion that played out in my family's life. As you will see in later chapters, God literally kept me alive.

By the beginning weeks of September of second grade it was clear I was going to need to have my tonsils out. The problem was that the iron in my blood was so low that they couldn't operate on me and that meant I would continue to be sick. It was quite a time trying to get my hemoglobin up high enough to do the surgery, I hated eating liver and broccoli and drinking that absolutely horrible liquid iron (barf). And even more than that, I hated the weekly blood draws to see how close I was getting to the "magic number" so that I could have the surgery. That very long set of stairs up to the lab gave me altogether too long to dread what I knew was going to happen next, and over and over and over again. I would start worrying as soon as they were done the deed about the next time I would have to be stuck. I would run and hide when it was time to go, but they always caught me and the consequences were painful.

The day finally came to have my surgery and I was afraid, but the nurses were nice to me and got me settled in my bed so that the surgery could be the next day. Auntie brought me to the hospital but had to leave as there were no visitors allowed overnight.

There was a little girl in the bed next to me who wasn't looking very happy. She had already had her surgery and every so often a nurse with a big needle came in and stuck her in her hiney with it. I couldn't understand why they had to keep hurting her like that. Evidently her situation didn't have that big an impact on me because I remember being in the playroom when a nice young man came in calling my name. I was so happy someone wanted to see me. Maybe I could get a toy or ice cream. My delight turned to terror and outright screaming as it took 6 people to hold me down to secure the blood sample they needed so that they could proceed with the surgery. Thankfully it was over soon and the next day they took me to surgery. I remember the yucky smelling stuff in the mask they put over my face before they operated, and that they insisted on putting it over my nose and mouth. As I struggled to get it off me they kept telling me it smelled like bubble gum. NOT. But, yucky or not it did the job and the next thing I remember was being in pain in my bed and vomiting; which, on the raw skin in my throat, burned like the fire of Hell I was being taught about in school every day. How to stop the pain? Painkillers injected into me which made me vomit. It really was a no win situation. I was alone, it was not visiting hours. I was so afraid. The nurses at the catholic hospital were sisters and they encouraged me to pray to Mary for help. I had put my scapular around my neck once I came out of surgery. All good catholic little girls wore one of the devotional artifacts with the belief that it would be of spiritual benefit to them. The Roman Catholic

Church considers it a sacramental, an item which bestows grace upon the wearer. (It consists of two small squares of cloth, wood or laminated paper, bearing religious images or texts, which are joined by two bands of cloth. The wearer places one square on the chest, rests the bands one on each shoulder and lets the second square drop down the back. Some scapulars have extra bands running under the arms and connecting the squares to prevent them from getting dislodged underneath the wearer's top layer of clothes. In lieu of it, the "scapular medal" may be worn, for good reason.)

NEAR DROWNING

In 1960 there was no "medical insurance" and between my mom's hospitalizations and illnesses, a parade of psychiatrists and specialists and my physical illnesses, my father had to work 16 hour days bringing glass gallons of bleach and ammonia to peoples' houses on his truck. He had to make the bleach in 12 foot tall cast iron vats from concentrated deliveries of chlorine. The ammonia came in 55 gallon drums and was diluted 5 gallons at a time because of its noxious, caustic characteristics and care was taken to not have vapors of both the bleach and ammonia filling the room at the same time because it made a poisonous gas which could kill you. They didn't use chemical masks for breathing back then either. Then they would wash the outside of the bottles and refill them, place them in cases and stack the cases in the truck for delivery. Labels were applied to new bottles and to existing bottles if they were no longer read-able after first being soaked in water to make them easy to scrape off with razor blades and rinsed.

This was done six days a week in all kinds of weather which meant measurable snow and ice from December or earlier until March or later. The street system there was city-like, numbered streets one direction and avenues the other. Houses were built on 40 x 60 lots with very little privacy between houses. They hadn't yet had the brainstorm of not putting windows on adjacent sides of the houses that faced each other. Actually, even if they did, it wouldn't be practical, because in that area there was no central air conditioning; indeed, very few people had even window air conditioners because they were considered a luxury that only rich people could afford. We had box fans and so did everyone else around us, hence needing windows on all sides of the house so that there would be air circulation throughout to help with the tremendous heat that visited us very occasionally during June, July and August, and the 80 – 85 degree weather the rest of the time. It was considered a "hot" summer if we had 15 days of temperatures over 90 degrees during those 3 months. Not 15 at a time; 15 spread out over the 3 months listed above.

We did have an above ground pool which helped make the summer more bearable for my cousins, my sister and I. Sometimes the girl in the house behind ours, "KD", came over and swam in our pool (even though she had her own pool). She was more of my sister's age or younger. One day I went over to swim in her pool with her and her father joined us (to make sure no one drowned). She didn't drown but I almost did. Her father had been drinking. I could smell the alcohol on his breath but didn't know at that age that alcohol impairs judgment and slows reflexes. Anyway, he was having a great time "dunking" me even though I was getting overloaded with pool water and the last time he dunked me that day he wouldn't let me up and I fought with everything in me to break free. As far as I remember I wasn't able to get free and was absolutely terrified that I was going to drown. At the very last second he let me up so I could get some air. I climbed out of that pool, ran out of the yard and never went back over there to swim. Definitely not if I knew her father was at home at all. It impacted me deeply, to this day (50 years more or less) I do not like water and especially I don't like horseplay in the water. I don't like watching my grandkids rough-house in the water. I am actually better since I had my inner healing for this event. Before that I couldn't tolerate being *in* water where I was not in absolute control. My kids' father had to play with them/go with them into the water/to the Water Park, etc.

There was one time during First Grade that I went to play with a friend after school and neglected to tell anyone where I was. When I got home I had a hysterical mother and a father who took down my underpants and put me over his knees and hit me so hard that I peed on him. That made him even more irate, because now there was a mess to clean up too.

I was always expected to know better; not knowing **anything** was a ticket to being called names or being hit or punished. An example of not knowing better was when I was walking down the hallway with my 3rd grade class and I was chewing on my fountain pen. Little did I know that it would break and I would wind up with ink all inside my mouth with nowhere to spit it out and nothing to wipe it on. I had to swallow it because if the sister in charge of our line found out what I had done I would get the inevitable verbal denigration and humiliation in front of all the other students and perhaps even be "blessed" with being slapped and/or dragged by my ear to the corner to stand with a dunce cap on. I *was* found out anyway with that ink in my mouth with the expected resulting discipline.

This was not the first time that I was humiliated in front of the class; I think 3rd grade was just a bad year for me. The sister I had was extremely demanding of all the students. One day I said the wrong thing and the sister brought me up to the front of the class and very deliberately smacked me in the face. She left red, puffy, welt marks on my face. I recall that we had had a science test and one of the questions was: "How many days are there in a week?" I wrote down 8 because I remembered the Beatles song "8 days a week". I didn't know the songwriters were purposely exaggerating the number of days in the week to facilitate a date with a certain female of whom they were admirers.

This same sister was also my teacher in the 7th grade and she was in charge of the choir for mass. I remember being up in the loft in the church where we were practicing; when I wasn't paying attention, I was talking to the girl next to me. The blessed sister was beside herself with me and told me to leave the choir and never come back. I think that was just a little overkill! Of course, the obligatory taunting and acerbic comments followed me out the door of the choir loft. That was sad because I had a good singing voice but lost the chance to try singing with it.

When I was 10, I begged to be able to choose my own clothing. I thought I was old enough and there was a "family" photo of me and my sister going to be taken. I didn't like the dress they wanted me to wear. It was a major victory when I was allowed, within reason, to decide what clothing I wanted to wear and to buy. Admittedly, it wasn't ***that*** big a big deal after all; we had to wear uniforms to school every day even though we hated them. It did decrease laundry and fights over what to wear! Other students wore the same as you and no one thought about stealing a classmate's apparel (not even the shoes, we all had to wear the same shoes too!!!!!). But you know that we female students found ways to obfuscate that dress code by rolling our skirts up among other things. When caught rolling we received wooden ruler slaps over the tops of our hands if the skirt didn't touch the ground when they made us kneel down.

We also delighted in stuffing our bras because we wanted the boys to see us and to drive the sisters crazy because we got to wear white semi-sheer blouses with those pleated navy blue plaid skirts. Some of the girls would add scarves around the neck to their uniforms; others wore lots of stuff in their hair. The sisters had to wear heavy, black, gown-like outfits that covered everything but their eyes, nose and mouth (some-what like the form fitted Hijab or Burka that Muslim women wear only more tailored).

When I wasn't in school, I spent a lot of time in front of the TV. It was my mother, teacher, friend and sister. It didn't yell at me or demand things of me; sometimes I wished it would. ***Any attention, even negative attention*** would have been better than being all alone in that house so many hours a day, every day. My other friend the radio put me to sleep every night. I was so glad the radio people knew I was alone and afraid. They were always there when I turned it on at bedtime; I found a couple of stations that I liked, some of which were just talk, talk, talk; but that was ok. At least they talked to me. One particular show called "Feminine Forum" gave me a lot of interesting things to think about because it was about women and I was going to become one soon.

Awake at night in my room, it was situated such that it faced the street and if I looked to the right I could see "Route X". Yes, the BIG highway. It always had cars going back and forth into the big city, even at 3 in the morning. This was in the late 50's, well before things gravitated to 24-hour everything. I was half afraid, half fascinated at that time of the morning. But I couldn't get back to sleep so I made the best of it. I wanted to get out the window, climb on the roof and jump down onto the soft green grass and go exploring the woods across the way but I was too young and afraid yet (5 years old?). So, I sat on the silver painted cast iron radiator below the windowsill and watched, smelled and listened for the blowing of the horns of the boats going under the drawbridge through town. I could also hear the train whistle and chugga-chugga sounds the trains made as they made their night runs into the big city. I wanted to ride on one of those trains and boats but the best I could hope for was hearing them in the distance. On these nights, the moon looked bigger than anything I had ever seen, sometimes yellow/orange just coming up over the housetops and tree tops beyond the woods and I could smell the creek which ran from town into the bay as the tide took the water out to sea each night. I felt like I was getting away with murder being able to do these activities in the wee hours of the morning while everyone else slept.

In the daytime I liked to read and so I spent a lot of time walking to the library to get books to help fill the time. I read books about candy stripers and nurses. It was an extra special pleasure when I was able to participate in the Recreation Department's summer program; under the pavilion in the new park that was built right down the street in the very same woods I used to watch from my window when I was awake at night. We made mosaic ashtrays and ceramic figurines which I was able to paint. I actually did something that came out nice. I wish I would have kept it for a good memory, but I never thought it would be one of the few things I ever did that was fun and showed that I had some kind of ability or talent.

I wanted to be a doctor when I grew up. I watched Dr. Kildare and Dr. Casey on TV. I had found a TV show on public television that we were able to receive because we lived by a big city; that had Dr. Robert Debakey transplanting the first artificial heart, the Jarvick 7, but I couldn't find books about doctors back then. I got to know the librarians who worked there; they were nice to me most of the time.

My mom liked car rides. Every Sunday after church we would go riding in the car with my dad. No seatbelts in 1960 so my sister and I lay in the back of the maroon Ford station wagon and played. My dad would take my mom and us out to a fancy Italian Restaurant where the people knew him by name; they even knew us kids by name (They used the bleach he delivered to them to clean the dishes and pots in the kitchen). I would have spaghetti and meatballs and a small portion of specially sweetened vanilla ice cream with shredded almond coating and a cherry on top, called a tortoni for dessert. My dad always had a sizzling steak with buttered noodles, definitely an oddity in an Italian Restaurant. We kids were always on our best behavior. My dad continued to take us there even after my mom no longer lived in our home. I'm thankful he HAD to eat and didn't like to cook every day.

My sister and I did not play together much growing up because of logistics, but my love of the family station wagon gave us fantasy time as we imagined (or were really) in faraway places. My mom loved to travel and was always trying to talk my dad into taking her places. When I was 10 my mom got her wish. The "powers that be" determined I was old enough to take care of my mother and sister (age 5); so we took the bus to a big resort town to stay for a week. On the first day both my mother and sister got so sunburned that they had sun poisoning and I was left trying to figure out what to do. My mother didn't want to do anything but cry, and my sister was in a lot of pain. Finally, I had to call my dad and have him drive that long distance to bring us home because my mom would not take the bus back home. I had failed and it cost my mom and sister terrible pain and suffering. My dad was not pleased either, he did not send me anywhere out of town with my mom and sister without another adult ever again.

Auntie and Unc lived on the bottom floor of the two-family house that my father and Auntie were given by their father when he and his wife retired and moved far away. Auntie wound up providing much of the care that I needed at her own sacrifice as well as taking care of her own children, my sister and my mother. Considering that the family she and my father grew up in didn't teach them how to show love and didn't speak of it for the most part, she really excelled at everything with so many responsibilities. As soon as I could figure out how to do something from watching someone else do it I took over doing it. It did have to be done exactly as they did it or I had to do it again or was forbidden to do it at all. Eventually I began to help take care of my sister and mother.

I can see in my mind's eye a single school photo in which my hair was standing up on end in some places; evidently I had also tried my hand at haircutting. My teeth were a squished mess of twisted and fang-like projections in my mouth, and, of course, I had too big a smile for the size of my jaw. I wore a maroon jumper with a white blouse and crisscross tie. It was as ugly as you could get but that is what we all had to wear. I don't know if it had been ironed that day or if it was even clean. The fact that I was wearing the maroon jumper means I was in 4th grade or younger as the 5th grade girls began wearing the blue plaid uniforms. Sometimes I was able to "sneak" out in the mornings without my auntie's inspection and this photo was the result of succeeding. I was so proud of myself at the time. I wince and feel sorry for that girl when I see that photo now.

Many, many years later when my father died, his wife gave me a photo album of sorts with black and white pictures of me as a young child with my parents and grandparents Nana and Bebop as well as Auntie and Unc. I couldn't deny they were me, but nothing "made the light go on" in my brain. This was one more example of my "putting forward" another part of me to deal with life at that time (Dissociative Identity Disorder). I was very thrilled to get those photos even if I was 45 years old. Up to this point I literally had nothing in the way of photos from my childhood because they were too low on the priority list of life. Things like food and shelter had to be taken care of first. Auntie and Unc had an 8mm home movie camera (no sound, this was the 60's) and I suppose that my father thought all the movies they took were more than enough to satisfy us (my sister and I *were* in many of them). I still don't have any of those reels; they are in Auntie's basement. It was God's doing that I wound up with that 11 x 15 of my sister and me, the one I was allowed to choose my dress for when I was 10, because after my father died his wife wanted to keep that picture of us girls and all the other ones too. She had no business trying to take those photos, we were not her children and I had a mother who would have loved to have had them were it possible in the nursing home where she was. I could see my auntie possibly keeping them because we were her nieces but my father's wife, nuh uh. She had four children of her own, 3 of them daughters. She had plenty of pictures of them, which should have been enough. Some day maybe I'll get copies of Auntie's movies, but it was way too late for my sister who died at the age of 34 in 1993.

In the summertime my father took me with him to deliver bleach to his customers on his big truck. I felt so special, I was his helper, ME!!!!! All of his customers were such nice ladies; many of them invited me in for a drink or gave me candy (slowing my dad down so we would either get less done or have to work later to finish each day). There was a sliding side door that my dad left open so that it wouldn't be so hot in the truck; there was no air conditioning, for the most part we didn't need it where we lived. Of course, there were the inevitable potty breaks; funny, I don't remember my father ever having used a bathroom! I'm sure he relieved himself somehow. We would stop at the same diner everyday for break-fast and then take lunch at a privately owned sand-wich shop or "deli" as we called them back then in whatever town we were in each day. Every deli was privately owned because where we lived the towns were 1 mile square or smaller. Everyone knew everyone else. Sitting out in the yard was standard as well as talking to the neighbors when the weather was nice. There was quite a sense of community which I miss where I live now. Here we are all spread out with a main highway running along the front of the property.

My father and Unc loaded their trucks at the "shop" where the vats were every day and the diner we ate in was two blocks away. Of course, we had the same waitress everyday and she loved to see me.

I found out the hard way that even if I didn't do something bad, other kids could lie and say I did and they would be believed and I wouldn't. I wound up being beaten many times because it was more expedient to beat me than work with my perceived misbehavior so I could improve. One day my Unc didn't believe what I said; and took me downstairs in the basement and put lye soap in my mouth. I wasn't strong enough to get loose and I could barely breathe it burned so badly. I swore I wouldn't lie ever again so that the punishment would end and I ran to rinse my mouth out where my uncle couldn't see me. I threw up because I wound up getting some of it down my throat with my screaming and trying to get loose. This event was especially disturbing because I didn't know my uncle very well, he wasn't at home much and when he was home he had his own kids to worry about. For some reason that day I wound up with him. I HAD NOT done what I was accused of and wasn't lying, not that that made any difference. It is very common for children with Dissociative Identity Disorder to be accused of lying simply by the fact that the presenting person WASN'T the one who told the lie or did the bad deed, but the whole system pays in this case.

I do recall having a housekeeper coming to our house each day for some period of time to help with my sister, the housework, and maybe even meals. I did not like her, she was all business. I wanted to do my own thing at 8 years old. This did NOT include having to clean my room all the time. This isn't surprising because by age 10 I was cleaning and helping take care of my sister when my mother was away sick. Sometimes I was "farmed out" to various relatives to be taken care of while my mom was in the hospital; one of which was my "Aunt M". Her son was in my 1st grade class with me and even though they lived in the next town, it was ok, because it was a private school and students from all over attended there. Her husband was in the car business and that atmosphere provided much for my imagination to use to stay busy. My sister did not go with me. I don't know what they did with her actually. I just knew that I was a "handful", too much for my mother to handle, and too young to be left alone yet. I suspect I don't remember much of my sister being around because she was downstairs with my aunt a lot of the time; (her two children were closer in age to my sister than I was. They were, in fact, younger than I was). I was a "tomboy" anyway. Both the fact that my father would have preferred a boy if he had gotten stuck with a kid and my inherent nature contributed to my down- to- earth quality, not "feminine" in any way I could get away with. I climbed trees, played kick ball, tag, rode my bike just like the boys. Just because I played like a boy and played with the boys does not mean *they* liked it; they were mean to me on many occasions. I did receive "physical medals" for my skill in those activities; you can still see where the barbed wire fence and I had a disagreement; it won. The marks are on my thighs and knees.

The summer when I was 8, I had somehow contracted ringworm on my skin which is contagious and impossible to hide in the summer. Its visibility resulted in being told that I had cooties. The boys all consistently ran away from me even as far as around the block and hid to lose me. The girls were equally vicious, running away and laughing at me. Even though the ringworm went away, the kids never forgot I had cooties and they continued to call me that for a long, long time.

I guess that year wasn't the best year for me either because one day all of the class had to go see the nurse. The nurse looked at my head. She pushed the hair all around (it was "styled" in what we would call now a "page boy"). Everyone had their turn and then it was back to class as usual. When I got home that day I was called a dirty little girl because I had bugs in my hair. They pulled me over the top of newspaper on our kitchen table and used this very tight comb to rip through my hair. It felt like they were trying to dig holes in my head. Every so often I would hear a plop and a moan of disgust from my father as Auntie combed the bugs out. Then I had to have this kerosene type "shampoo" on my hair to kill the eggs. The next day I got a haircut which left me looking like a boy. There was very little hair left on my head. Somehow all my classmates knew I had had bugs and they all laughed and ran away from me. They called me mean names for quite a while. It didn't help that my classmates were the same kids from Kindergarten until 8th grade (minus new admissions and those who "left", i.e. moved or transferred to public school).

Of course my little sister (all of 3 years old) had bugs too and they "scalped" her at the hair cutting place the next day. All that beautifully reddish-brown "Orphan Annie" hair on the floor beneath the chair she sat in. I got blamed for that too. They thought that I should have known better and kept myself clean.

My own oldest child came home from public school with lice 18 years later and I just went and got the shampoo and washed her hair. Unfortunately I didn't get the "nits" as the nurse showed me when I tried to bring my child to school the next day, so I had to take her to a haircutter so they could cut her hair very short, but at least she wasn't called ugly or ridiculed for something that is *a public health nuisance found in schools, not her fault or mine either for that matter.*

Once I went through my experience I put all the combs and brushes in my house into an ammonia wash and soak once a week so that I wouldn't wind up that way ever again. Funny, even with that hygienic routine I wound up with lice again after a visit to a holistic doctor/clinic where they took a hair sample to test for heavy metals. I was furious I wound up with that from there and I let them know pronto. Thankfully, none of my own children got them from me. Maybe ammonia wasn't the right chemical to use to kill nits after all. I just had been lucky all that time to not have been exposed to them again!!

When girls became more of interest to me, I was a little older, 11; we had a "fort" in the woods where we held our "secret" club meetings. We didn't want any other kids in our club; therefore, it became "secret". We had contraband; cigarettes and stolen records of the songs we heard on our transistor radios, matches to light those cigarettes and to make campfires. There were big "cat tails" there, those reed type plants with big brown fuzzy hot dog looking parts on top. I never found out the real name of them, we just lit them on fire and smelled them. Because my father knew the editor of our little town's weekly newspaper very well because of the leisure activity he was the boss of, I was able to get one of their photographers to take a picture of us girls and our fort. I was so proud.

It was an exclusive club and my membership was paid in cold cash or stolen goods from the supermarket (until I got caught) and from the Drug Store next door (which in those days had a soda fountain in addition to the usual pharmacy type items and services). Our "fort" was actually an empty lot which was next to the public park; years after we grew up it was filled in with 2 multifamily houses. Every time I walk past it now I still remember our "fort". Of course, most of the time we spent in the fort was in the summer, it got too cold and there was too much school and home-work and chores during the other seasons. The girls I was with were sisters who attended school with me who were living with their Aunts who spoke English and their grandmother who only spoke her native tongue, Lithuanian. Several of the other girls on the block were forbidden to "play" with me; I don't know why they weren't. I guessed it was because I was a "wild child" or bad or had a sick mother, or all of the above. It was all so confusing to me.

Another "thing" we girls did was play doctor; yep, the inevitable exploration of the female form by other females. It was the usual 3 of us; but one day another girl who was older than us by a couple of years wandered over to us at school and asked if she could be friends with us. Evidently she had just moved to our town and lived only a few houses down the street from me. This was the first time anybody wanted to be my friend!!! Sure. Well, we took her up to my bedroom at which time we asked her to take off her clothes and she was too afraid. So she just watched the rest of us use pencils with erasers to explore usually covered body cavities and areas. I didn't know it was wrong and it felt good. I came to find out that it wasn't good to do because several days later I went over to where our new "friend" lived; with her grandparents, (none of us kids knew where her parents were), and when the door opened there was this mean and ugly little gray haired woman screaming at me how I was a dirty little girl and I would burn in hell for asking her granddaughter to play "show and tell". And then she exposed her grand-daughter's secret places and screamed, "There, is that what you wanted to see?" Of course our "friend" started crying and I wanted to die for the beating she was going to get. We girls never saw her again and

I was left wondering whether my hands were going to catch fire. If this wicked grandmother went to my father I would join in the "getting a beating" club for this activity. To my memory, he never did find out, but Auntie did. I don't know if she told my dad and told him not to punish me or if she kept my secret but I sure was glad for whatever the reason was that he didn't punish me.

Evidently my riding on the truck with my dad in the summer became "old hat" and so the summer when I was 9 I went to "day camp". It was a YMCA/YWCA camp where I would leave each morning at 7:00 a.m.; and return each night at 6 p.m. because they didn't provide dinner, just lunch. To get the bus, I walked up two blocks to the highway. I went by myself, no adult with me. It was an hour drive each way but that didn't bother me, I was so excited to go and there were other kids there; kids that wouldn't know me. Maybe I could make a friend.

I guess it wasn't meant to be because one more time I found myself in the girl's bathroom/changing area and I went to go in a stall I thought was empty and happened upon an older girl who was fully developed. I screamed and ran out of the building I was so frightened and expecting retribution for my "mistake". The girl who was getting changed was NOT happy with me, but was evidently old enough to realize that I didn't know what I was doing and didn't confront me.

I remember that we had an overnight campout toward the end of the 8 weeks of day camp. School was going to start back up soon and so camp was coming to an end. We had a big cookout for our parents and families. I think my father did not attend but my Aunt did and was very late; I thought my father wasn't impressed with me or what I had done. The campout part was scary because we had to put up tents and sleep in them in the woods with no lights anywhere and no bathroom nearby. I was afraid to be in the woods with people I didn't really think could take care of an emergency like a bear or something in the middle of the night.

As the weeks went from 1st to 8th, progress reports were sent home to the parents and I don't know WHAT they put on mine but it wasn't good. My care-givers at home wouldn't let me see what they said, just told me that it was bad. How could I improve or correct what was wrong if no one would tell me what that was? This just cemented the idea in my mind that something was *"wrong"* with me, something that couldn't be fixed, after all; even the camp counselors saw it too and sent home a report confirming it.

On Saturdays there wasn't camp so I went down to the new park in town that I could see from my bedroom and chose a swing to swing on. I sat on it and laid straight back while I pumped with my feet and it was such a cool sensation seeing everything upside down. I used to watch the clouds roll by and would guess what item they looked like. After a while that got boring so I decided to stand up on the swing. Maybe I could swing as high as I had seen the older kids do. Uh, no. I fell face first onto the railroad tie that separated the grass from the sand that was under the swings for just such an occasion. Too bad

I missed the sand and hit the divider. I went home screaming in pain and bleeding out my nose. I was given ice and an aspirin and told to go lay down.

Twenty years later I had surgery to correct the deviated septum that resulted from that fall. I had been very sick with continuous sinus infections while carrying my son. After he was born I took college classes in Anatomy and Physiology and that was when I became aware that possibly something was wrong with my nose.

I went to the Ear, Nose, and Throat Specialist that took care of my kids to find out about the problem with my nose. I'll never forget the first time that I went to this doctor with my middle child. I had an opinion of what he would look like based on his name. No one had told me what he looked like. So, we are sitting there waiting for him to come in and in comes some guy in scrubs. Tall, young, nice tan, thick black hair, beautiful smile, and handsome; a doctor "McDreamy" before his time. I was sure this was either his partner or someone who took a wrong turn in the hallway and wound up here. The doctor I was waiting for would be short, old, with white hair and a bald spot, plenty of wrinkles, long white beard and even perhaps a hunch back. I was shocked when he said his name. This couldn't be the doctor!!!! He asked why so many questions and I told him what I had expected he would look like. He thought that was funny. What was funny was that his partner that I met later would look like my imagined doctor in 20 years as he already had the beard, a small hunch back, thinning hair, etc.

Young, "Dr. McDreamy" confirmed that the reason I breathed out of my mouth was because one side of my nose was almost completely blocked by the septum having been pushed over from the other side of the nose. He asked me if I had been in a fight, I thought that was really funny; I told him that I had fallen when I was 8 or 9 and remember bleeding and pain. He said that was what had done the damage. I had the surgery and it is a good thing they didn't tell me how difficult recovery was. I probably would not have had the surgery, thank you very much!!!! As it was, I wound up being one of the chosen few. Because I was a nursing student, one of the bones he had to trim the scar tissue off had not clotted properly and so I was coughing and gagging when I tried to eat post-op and if I coughed hard enough I would start bleeding. I had started bleeding when they removed the packing and was told that it was normal, put ice on it. Maybe I was superstitious but this sounded way too familiar to me. Something was wrong, I knew it. After a week at home I had to go into the surgeon's office to have the splinting removed from my nose. When I reached home I had blood in my mouth again. I rinsed my mouth and tried to go on with life, after all, I had 3 young children to take care of.

Several days of this bleeding went on and I was getting really tired of the gagging and coughing and now vomiting from the coughing that I called the surgeon's office and told them I needed to be seen. They told me the doctor was in surgery to go to the ER of the hospital that he was operating in currently. I had to find someone to watch my youngest children because they weren't in school yet and I had to have my husband drive me because now I had to hold a bath towel underneath my nose to catch the blood. YES, I *was icing it*, had been icing it and I still bled. When I arrived there I was agitated because I knew something wasn't right and nothing that had happened in connection with this surgery was pleasant so far, I figured it would get worse before it got better. It was a long time waiting for the doctor to finish his surgery and a nurse would check on my bleeding every so many minutes. They gave me an emesis basin for the blood to run into so they could measure how much blood I was actually losing. Once I arrived in the ER the bleeding seemed to slow down some, I guess I relaxed a little knowing someone there would help me. My husband, on the other hand, was getting more and more agitated because he was missing work and was afraid something else was wrong with me. I was so worried about his anger at me for having this problem that it showed in my pulse and blood pressure. The nurse asked me what was wrong and I told her that my husband was going to kill me for screwing up his day. Next thing I knew she came back to me with something in a needle that she put into my IV. The anxiety lessened and I really didn't care anymore what my husband was feeling and for that matter what I was feeling!!!! Evidently, though, the doctor did because he was there shortly with his partner ENT doctor. I didn't realize that the trickle had become more like a river and so the nurse told the doctor and he came down right away. In order to see what was going on that far in and up my nose he had to put the gurney with the feet up and the head down. He was standing bent over with a "miner's light" on his head straining to see what the problem was. That was when he saw the bone with no clot on it and said ONLY nursing students, physician's family members, etc. have these kinds of problems (which really is an old wives tale); just another day at the hospital for him. I started to panic again when I thought he was going to send me home again. I really thought I needed some rest and time to heal and at home that wasn't going to happen. He admitted me after he packed my nose back up, splinted it again, and gave me a shot of pain medicine from which I blissfully and thankfully passed out. I praised God for how He knew what I needed when I didn't even know what I needed and He took care of it before I even knew I had a need. (Matthew 6:8b – For your Father knows what you need before you ask him). I remember our Pastor arriving and his praying for me but that was only later, after he reminded me of what he did!!! Let someone else take care of my very angry husband, I'm going nite-nite. This time it was 10 days in the hospital before they removed the packing and there was NO bleeding then or ever again in connection with my deviated septum. Did I finish my nurses training? I'll tell that part of the story later.

THE BULLY

I even managed to avail myself of my own personal bully, "JW". I guess she was in high school or maybe I was younger and she was in the 5th – 8th grade. All I remember was that she would "hide" behind objects on the block I had to walk by to get home from school every day and would pop out and threaten to beat me up. She even had her own name for me "UNA" which she said denoted animal or insect life, not human life. I sure was hoping that she would move or go to a different school or something so that I didn't have to fear her threats every day. No, I couldn't tell anyone about her, I had experienced being in a fight with a very mad contemporary already and I did not want to repeat the experience. She said if I did tell anyone she would bring some friends with her to beat me up. I guess her class schedule or something changed because I believe I had a short period of time when she wasn't around after school and I could walk home without fear of a beating.

Turned out she was, indeed, older than me and where she went was public high school, which let out later than our grade school. I didn't care what the reason was, I was just glad for the reprieve. That reprieve ended when I became a freshman in the same high school. She was in my gym class. Here they mixed grades in gym and I had never been exposed to gym, our private school didn't have gym classes, no less mixed gym classes. I had not seen "JW" out in the gym but when I came back to the locker area to get changed back into street clothes so I wouldn't miss my next class she came up behind me with her familiar welcoming phrase: "Hey there, Una!!!". I was hoping I was hallucinating from over-exertion never having had a gym class before. Maybe she wasn't real. I turned around and it WAS her. I was speechless. She wasn't. She told me that next gym period she was going to get some of her fellow senior girls to throw me in the shower after they had made me take my clothes off. I don't know about your high school gym class but in ours no one used the communal showers after gym class. Maybe they were used after cheerleader practice and so forth but not after gym class. I sure didn't want to use them. I didn't want to be forced to remove my clothes in front of all different classes and ages of girls. I finished up changing and left as fast as I could. "JW" made sure to remind me about my next gym class and the impending humiliation. What if it was that time of the month? I would simply die, nothing else. I really didn't know what to do. I could not miss class, I would get "cuts" which would drop my grade and label me as a bad student; but I couldn't attend either because "JW" would carry through on her threat now that she had the "senior" girls with her. Freshmen were the scourge of the earth in the first place, just for having been born. We existed to serve all the upperclassmen, sophomore and up; seniors are untouchable.

I wasn't quite sure what a Guidance Counselor was, but I was about to find out. I made an appointment and got a permission slip to be late to class to go there. The woman there was quite cordial. I explained my problem in as few words as possible and asked her what to do. She assured me that no one was going to force me to get naked in the showers and gave me a "skip class" excuse for the next gym class. The following class I went back and "JW" and her friends just ignored me. I was so relieved. I can't ever prove it, but I believe she and her "senior" girls got called into the Guidance Office and told to cut it out and leave me alone or else there would be unpleasant consequences for them. God arranged this for me too and He deserves all the praise for it.

Once I was promoted to the 5th grade, I began stealing candy from the town supermarket and of course, got caught. I was lucky because the store manager called my mom, not knowing she really wasn't "all there" and she came down and got me. He said I could never return to that store again to shop and told me I was lucky he didn't get the police in there to take me to jail. No doubt I deserved whatever came my way but it still left enough fear to cause nightmares over and over and over again about being taken to jail for real. Or about my dad finding out what I had done and the beating that would follow. At around the same age I began stealing from my mother's "box". She put the cash my dad gave her each week for the "household" in the box and would take out what she needed as she needed it. I didn't care that she would get in trouble with my dad because she was short money; I never admitted I took what I wanted. I was given no allowance and all the neighborhood kids had money, so I wanted some too. Eventually I stopped taking money because my father stopped giving my mother money. Eventually, she was relocated out of our house.

THE DENTIST

I have always had trouble with anything that could possibly be physically painful since my tonsillectomy in 2nd grade. Anytime the nurse came to our classroom I knew I was in for pain of some type and there was no one there to help me escape it. I clearly remember getting my smallpox vaccination at school, yearly Schick tests for Tuberculosis, hearing and vision tests; for which I was thankful because I couldn't see like the other children did, I had to sit close up to see the board. My eyesight problem wasn't discovered until the 2nd grade after I returned from my tonsil surgery, I was probably absent for the previous two years' vision screenings because I was sick.

If there was anything I hated more than doctors it was dentists. I know that no one enjoys the dentist even now in the 21st Century but at least you can get treated without tremendous pain. I think you can paint the picture of the 1960's dentist visit. For me, it was brutal. I had a tremendous amount of decay from not being instructed how to brush my teeth and from not brushing them anyway if I did know how. I went from one dentist to the next being tortured as I screamed in pain. It only got worse the more I struggled but I couldn't help it. Because of that I went around with terrible tooth aches which resulted in my losing teeth that were too far gone to repair at a very young age. Once I was older I just refused to go to the dentist for other than cleanings and those only IF the hygienist was gentle with me. It took me until I was 14 to go to yet another new dentist and I was informed that I needed braces to bring those fangs down out of the top of my gums in the front. I also did not have enough room for all my teeth so as the wisdom teeth started to push up I was in a lot of pain. I had four first molars removed by the most wonderful, kind, painless, orthodontist that existed in 1970. I asked him if he could do my fillings too!!!! I actually looked forward to my monthly braces adjustments because he was such a good practitioner. I got my braces off the week before senior pictures.

I wish I could say that that was the end of my dental phobia and torture but it wasn't. If I wanted to keep my now straight and beautiful teeth in my mouth I had to see a dentist to get my teeth cleaned and x-rayed every year. Neither of my parents kept their teeth, they wound up with dentures that neither one of them were able to eat with. I think the "handwriting on the wall" for me was clear. I had to find the courage to go to a new dentist that someone in my dad's business had used for herself and so I went. He drilled my back bottom molar even though I kept telling him that he was hurting me. It was so deep that he put in a temporary to be removed and filled permanently after a round of antibiotics. I never was able to summon the courage to return for the final treatment of that tooth and several years later went to a dental surgeon and had it removed; only to stop the pain in my mouth. As a result, the teeth that were so beautifully straightened and aligned started to slide in my gums to fill up the space that the extracted tooth used to occupy. I have spaces between my teeth now that don't belong there. I was fitted for a retainer when the braces were removed and, for a while, I wore it every night when I went to bed. But, it was so hot and dry because of the enclosed steam heat system. I also breathed through my mouth because my septum was deviated in my nose and I didn't know it back then. The thermostat for both floors was located downstairs where they had 11 foot ceilings; ours were 8 foot so it was HOT in our apartment. In fact, each room had a window open about an inch until days of the summer heat just so we could sleep in my house. My mouth wound up feeling like cotton was stuffed in it and I had to pull the retainer off my gums every morning. Eventually it broke from the strain and I knew my father couldn't afford to buy me a new one, so I went without.

THE FIRST SEXUAL ABUSE

While we are talking about physically painful events, I had an event that left a tremendous amount of fear and shame in me; namely, when I began to mature into a woman from a girl. I used to wear a sky blue baby doll pajama made of some type of sheer cotton material (remember, no air conditioning so it was hot) around the house in preparation for bed. My father and Unc would sit together in our living room watching the "Million Dollar Movie" on TV. It was a big deal in the 1960's before cable came into existence. Anyway, if they thought that the movie du jour was not "too old" for me I was allowed to stay up to watch it with them. One night Auntie came up because she needed something from Unc and saw my top and started yelling at me that I was a not nice girl for wearing that top because it was see through; she implied that I knew better and did it to show off my young nubile body to her husband. The men could see my developing body and indeed they did every night for a long time before my auntie informed me I should not do that. The net effect of that incident was that I wore sweaters in 90 plus degree weather to make sure I was covered enough that nothing would show. I was only 10 or 11 at the time and I didn't know any better. I felt deeply ashamed and stupid.

It appears I took my stupidity with me wherever I went. By 6th grade the girls at school had had more than enough of me so I hung around the boys. For some reason they appreciated me. By then I was looking like a woman but most of them were still boys. I didn't know the difference at that point. One of the boys was somewhat shy and stayed away from the rest of the boys who pretty well treated him like the girls treated me. We wound up talking to each other every day at recess and lunch. We managed to find a staircase on the side of the school building where the church was connected internally and we would sit there unseen. After a period of time I became more interested in his family. He spoke French and his parents were from France. He had a younger sister also who lived at home. Well, since it was so deadly boring at my house, I would walk the two miles to his house after school. His parents worked so there wasn't anyone home most of the time, even his sister seemed to be there every day except the ones I visited. I was so happy to have anyone to talk to and spend time with that even though I thought it might not be a good thing to do; he and I played show and tell. I can't remember if he didn't have much to show or, once again, I was the only one to show, but the riot it produced at school when he started playing "macho man" because of what he had talked me into doing was awful. I was so ashamed again. I trusted him and he really didn't like me, he was just using me.

My schoolmates were so cruel with their hatred of me. They informed me that I had alligator hands and that they were ugly with hair growing on top of the fingers. For years I shaved my fingers and toes everyday and tried to keep them hidden inside my socks, sleeves or in sweater pockets (we were allowed to wear solid navy blue cardigans over our uniforms when it was cold; for me it was always cold). There was nothing "wrong" with my hands or toes. The fingers were short and fat and I had been cracking my knuckles for years causing them to appear bigger. I bit my nails until they bled so that was not very becoming. My "problem" was genetic. My dad had literally rock hard skin over his hands and he bit his nails too. I thought that his condition occurred because he was a chemical handler and worked out in the elements since he was 11. Perhaps his choice of occupation made his hands worse than they would have been, but the characteristics of his hands were dictated by heredity, his father had rough hand also. I found out later that my hands were perhaps not as pretty as the other girls, but I had strength in them; strength from hard work at my father's business washing bottles and scraping them and from waitressing later on when I was old enough to work legally.

That particular Christmas at school our teacher Mr. P decided to have a talent exhibition. By this point in my life I had been playing fife in that marching band for a few years and so I volunteered to play it for the class. The only thing was that I did do it with a record of the song on it so that it would hide any mistakes I might make. When the time came, they wanted me to play it without the recording and I wouldn't. They jeered at me for that.

Speaking of boys using me, by the time I got into 8th grade I suddenly began to exhibit the possibility I might have a brain. A fellow 8th grade boy approached me and asked me to go out with him. He asked me to come to his house (located up the block from mine) to meet his family and we could hang out there. I vaguely knew his sister, brother and mother from school and the extracurricular activity that both "BG" and I participated in. I went to his house, met his family and he told me that he was having trouble with a writing assignment or math assignment or maybe even both and couldn't leave until he was done. He asked if I could help him. I did, of course, help him that day and the day after and the day after that for quite a while. I had wanted to go somewhere else, do more than schoolwork and watch TV and so I asked him (that is a no-no also in 1968) if we could do something else. He said fine that he would come to my house and we could go to a movie. I got "cleaned up" and was waiting for his arrival. He was late. 15 minutes, 30 minutes, 45 minutes, one hour. If he didn't get there soon we wouldn't have any time to do anything else, no less the movie he talked about. I called his house finally and his brother told me that he had gone out with "JJ" (another girl) and

74

had never even mentioned me in the same sentence as "date".

I was pretty mad after that and so on the next school day I saw him and confronted him about not showing up and he started laughing at me saying he couldn't believe I was stupid enough to think he would go ANYWHERE with ME, Miss Ugly. He should talk, he strongly resembled Herman Munster!! Use me for school enough so that he would graduate, sure. But, date! He was beside himself with laughter and, of course, all the other boys and girls were just about rolling around on the ground laughing at me. It hurt, but worse than that I couldn't figure out what I was doing wrong that they all treated me so poorly. As I reflect on it, I don't think I was doing anything wrong other than trusting the wrong people; no, I was just a convenient target for their natural meanness and arrogance.

By the time I was in 8th grade I was spending my spare time with an older crowd of girls and boys. The band I was in was now an older band and many of the boys were juniors in school or older. There was one "boy" I met that I didn't know from school at all. I believe he was new to the band and he asked me to go to a dance with him. I did and during the dance he wanted to go outside for a break. While we were outside he maneuvered me to where we weren't very visible and began to kiss me. I wasn't sure I liked him enough for this kiss but I was absolutely sure I didn't like him enough when he put his hands up my blouse and started pulling my bra up out of the way of his hands. I wasn't polite; I grabbed his hands and pulled them out. I told him in no uncertain terms that I did not invite him to do that and that I WASN'T that type of girl and I didn't want anything else to do with him ever again. By this time in my life I wondered if I had a huge sign on me saying "ABUSE ME PLEASE". I found out later when I was going through inner healing and deliverance that there was indeed a "sign", one that every demon around me could see; indeed, instructing them to abuse me. After I confessed that I believed the lies of the demons and did not believe what God told me in His Word, The Bible. I renounced any vow or agreement made with the demonic realm concerning this area of sinful activity, and the appropriate inner healing of the wound from my childhood that led me to believe lies instead of God, that sign was removed by Jesus. No more was I abused physically once Jesus removed that sign. To Him is all the glory. Unfortunately, there were more physical abuse incidents between high school and 1999 which I will detail in future chapters.

A REAL LIVE PENIS

W e took overnight trips to competitions in far away places where we were all bussed and put up in hotel rooms. The inevitable drinking and partying took place while there. My father was around somewhere but I didn't see much of him. There was a huge boardwalk in the town where we had a competition once and so all the girls went out after dinner to have fun. I went with them the first night, but the second night I didn't want to do all that walking; particularly because we had a huge competition and then a long parade after that the next day. Even if I was on my last leg I had to do those events and do them perfectly so that we would win the trophy and make the adults happy (ok, maybe we would be happy too). So, I stayed behind and strayed over to one of the busses that had transported us. The door was open and I could hear voices inside. I knew there was supposed to be wine so I went in. I saw one of the older boys toward the back of the bus (he was so cute with dark, wavy hair, Irish looking face, looking younger than his stated age). There was someone there that I hadn't heard or seen from the outside but recognized once inside. They were drinking and seemed under the influence so I started to leave when the older one asked me to come back to their room at the hotel after dinner. I had such a crush on the "cute boy" that this sounded like a way to get closer to him. I arrived at the stated time and "cute boy" answered the door and let me in. The older boy was sitting there. I sat down and they started talking and offered me something to drink. We continued to talk when the older boy went into the bathroom. He called cutie over and the next thing I know good "Ole Boy" came out of the bathroom with his pants down and a full erection. I shrieked and went running for the door; they laughed so hard they could barely breathe. "Ole Boy" was saying: "I TOLD YOU she had never seen the real thing". I was now afraid of being raped so I kept running and stayed away from them the rest of the time we were there. I don't know if you caught the fact that I reacted with fear instead of curiosity of what a penis was and what do you do with it? By this time I had had the experience with my father and uncle about my being a slut for wearing that blue nightgown. I had felt exposed instead of protected and therefore any male was threatening to me because I knew what they wanted to do to me if they could and they would use "that thing", the penis to do it to me. I had read about what a man does with "that thing" in a medical home care book when I was 10 and it was disgusting and painful I thought. I also thought that I could get pregnant at any time without the benefit of sex like the Virgin Mary did. In my mind the two weren't connected. You can see the gaps caused by lack of communication and inability to ask questions when given only limited information on subjects like sex.

A year or two later I was at one of the indoor color guard contests that we competed in for 3 years and I had met a new guy. He was 21 and in the Air Force and I was maybe 13, no older. We had been seeing each other at the contests for a while then. He had been wearing his uniform and I liked that. We didn't do much but eat, watch the other bands compete; nothing exciting. We didn't do that on this day. He informed me that he had something really special to tell me and he couldn't do it where people were. Here I was thinking that maybe he was going to ask me to "go steady", I was so excited. He asked me to get in his car and so I did and we were off. He drove up to this building I didn't recognize and told me it was his friends' and he had left his "fill in the blank, I can't remember what" inside; that it might take a minute. Why don't I come in? Great, I thought. I was so proud, he was in the military and he liked me and was going out with me???? Whoopee. Not exactly. When he opened the door there was a bed and a kitchenette. He told me that he had been waiting all these weeks for this time for us to "do it". I told him I was NOT going to do anything with him without clothing on. He was obviously crestfallen but was willing to "dry hump" me. I didn't know what he was hoping to accomplish at that point, but the kissing was good. Then, suddenly, the door swung open and there were several of the boys and girls from the bands. They all cracked up laughing at my having this boy on top of me rubbing himself against me when they opened the door. I turned bright red and was so humiliated that I grabbed my stuff and went running out the door. I didn't even know how I was going to get back to the competition because he drove me here and I wasn't paying attention. I guess I got back ok because I'm here today!!! Once again God let this boy go only so far in his abuse of me, sparing me from much worse, and graciously healed me of the damage that had taken place by that boy at a later date.

There was another day 6 months later during band competition that I had a crush on a boy whose name I thought was "LP". I had only seen him from a distance but the girls with me told me who he was. Well, one of the girls in the color guard who was older than me invited me to come to her house where "LP" and several other boys in the band would be with their girls having a party. I said fine because I knew the girl and the rest of those who were to be in attendance. The way she explained it, I was to be with "LP". I got there early and yet everyone else was already there with the girls sitting on the laps of the boys. And there was "TP" sitting on "LP's" lap. Some other ugly boy was sitting alone and I was supposed to be with him. The drinking began and as time went on, the couples went off into the bedrooms to enjoy themselves. Needless to say I went in the room but did nothing other than tell whoever he was that I wasn't interested in what he had to offer.

By now I guess you could say there was a pattern of me liking some guy and his using/abusing me. Along with that came a "sterling" reputation of being a whoooa (shortened form of the word whore), slut, boy crazy, cheap trick, best blow job, etc. etc. The hard part was that I didn't do anything more than kiss. I didn't even know WHAT a blow job was!!!

Where was God in all this? At that time in my life my opinion of God was that He was impossible to please and very demanding but I still hoped I had a chance of getting into heaven.

There was a day in May, Assumption Thursday, a high holy day for the church; a celebration every year of the day when Mary ascended in bodily form into heaven because they believe she was the *sinless* mother of God. Every year I looked forward to it. The weather was always wonderfully sunny and warm (for that area at that time of year). The church was decorated with tons of lovely flowers and many, many lit candles. The purple Lenten covers placed at the beginning of lent as a sign of repentance of sin were removed after Easter from all the statues of the saints and Mary.

It was a high mass so there was a lot more singing; the entire school went to the mass, from 1st to 8th grades that made it quite a bunch. And by this time in my life, the Vatican II had met and the mass was actually being conducted in English instead of Latin. We all took communion that day and school was dismissed after the mass. This mass was in addition to the mass all of the students attended once a week as a school body. This mass was only open to the students, no outsiders.

I really loved God and wanted to be near Him despite the images I was given by those teaching me. I would do things the other kids didn't because of my devotion. One such thing was doing the "Stations of the Cross". In the sanctuary of our church (whether they have this in every church I don't know), there were 14 large non-paper pictures of Jesus hung on the side walls of the outside pews equidistant so that they were evenly spaced around the entire outside of the pews. The first one showed Jesus going from where He was convicted of His claim of being God to the final one which was His crucifixion. You notice I didn't say His resurrection. In the Catholic church Jesus is still on the cross, dying every time Mass is celebrated. Evidently once wasn't enough to satisfy God's requirements of payment for sin in their way of thinking. That is why you will see crucifixes in the Catholic churches and any other place a Catholic person might have one with Jesus still on it.

The summer between 8th grade and High School I will refer to as "The Middle Summer". A lot happened that summer, but the biggest thing was my dad's moving my mom out of our home into her parents' home (Nana and Bebop's). He felt that she was a bad influence for us girls because of her mental problems and her hygiene problem. I don't know if he finally felt he could do this because I was old enough to take care of myself and my sister or if he had had his conscience eased by several conversations with two different priests about his moral obligation to her; but my mom's anxiety ratcheted up a notch when Bebop "retired" and moved with Nana 50 miles away from us into the country. It facilitated another stay for my mom in the psychiatric hospital for shock treatments and to get her medications corrected. No more daily bus rides to visit Nana and Bebop, they couldn't come over by us even if they wanted to (I don't recall them coming to our house very often, it was usually us going there anyway, I don't believe my grandmother even had a driver's license.) My mom got more and more frantic every day without them close by and was becoming more of a burden for my father. So he took her to their retirement house 50 miles away and left her there when she came home from the hospital in stable condition.

It all started when my mom was 17 and was in a car accident with a bus. Even though the property damage to the car was minor and she had no physical injuries, she had what was the first of many such episodes all throughout my childhood designated a "nervous breakdown". Of course, I wasn't born yet so my information on what went on with my mother came from auntie and my dad. My mom was a beautiful woman and a very intelligent woman my father said, and when I saw photos of her at age 17 and up they bore out that truth. She was at the top of her high school class and became a proficient legal secretary upon completion of high school. She worked at that until she married my dad at age 21. At age 30 when my sister was born my mom showed the physical evidence of having carried two children which she was terrified of having all by herself while my dad "worked". She had given up trying to please him because when she did try, he would reject her. She was in and out of psychiatric hospitals where they tried valiantly with what they knew at the time to fix her and if that wasn't possible they at least tried to get her able to function somewhat because she had two young children at home. They had given her "shock treatments" because all she would do was sit in a chair and rock; back and forth day after day. Never bathing, eating or even talking, just that blank stare and the rocking. I thought that the shock treatments had ruined her brain because she had significant short term memory loss; and when I tried to talk to her she wouldn't understand me; and kept asking me the same questions over and over and over again even though I had answered her with the same answer every time. Later on I learned that the treatments had worked to some degree because she had been talking to "friends of the family" where she and my dad would go play the card game Canasta. We kids got to go and play with whatever age and sex childen were there at the time. I so looked forward to being able to play with anyone anywhere, but if there was ever a "problem" between me and the friends' children; I got punished without their even listening to my side of the story. Even though the kids at school were in the "in crowd" and I wasn't, the names they called me at least acknowledged I existed.

Once my mom was no longer in the home my dad took me to that diner to have Sunday breakfast and then we would go food shopping in the area nearby. I felt so big and so important! At home I could walk through the park directly to the grocery store and pick up whatever my dad told me to get and bring it home and most days that is what I did once I learned how to count money.

I had a lot of anger towards my father at that point because he took away my patsy, my easy touch, my ability to manipulate to get most whatever I wanted. But as I grew older and started learning about the world we lived in I became enraged at him for dumping her. Yes, she had problems, problems that didn't seem to have a solution; but to drive her 50 miles away without telling her he was going to leave her there with her parents?? *So* unfair and selfish, self serving. And so began the war between my dad and me. Once I got out of that "nunnery" (grade school) and went to public high school I began to hear *normal* people's thoughts and ideas. I realized how warped our lives were. I was determined to start over and become someone else. This led to my challenging my father's way of doing things. He definitely didn't need or want that. He would say to me: "Who died and left you boss?" if I dared question him about something he had said no to or something he said or did that I found out wasn't honest. He wouldn't ever explain himself, it became "because I said so"; and "do what I say not what I do." And "Who are you Mother Teresa"? Believe it or not, he started coming home at night even less than he previously had. He bowled 4 nights a week and came home under the influence of alcohol most nights. I would still be awake at 10 pm and I would see him taking what looked like a handful of Vanquish (headache remedy) knowing he had alcohol in him. I feared he would die and I would be left all alone and then I WOULD wind up in that Bad Girl's Home that I thought I had skimmed by because I got smarter in my actions; there simply wasn't anywhere else to go. I never questioned it before but right now I wonder why I didn't think my Auntie and Unc would take care of us if something happened to my dad too. Again, this reveals what I didn't cognitively understand but intuitively knew – I was not worth the air I consumed. Air someone more worthy could breathe if I wasn't here.

I began having trouble sleeping at night because I was afraid my dad would die; and then I became afraid *to* sleep because my dad would come in drunk once I was asleep and start screaming at me for not having put the dishes away before I went to bed or anything else he found that angered him. He took an entire drain board of clean, dry dishes and threw it out the second story hall window of our house one night during one of his rages; with the houses so close all the neighbors heard it too. But, there was no escape. I lived there and had to figure out how to survive. I began to learn how to sense what mood my father was in by the way he looked, talked, sounded or didn't, etc. I needed to do this in order to stay out of the range of his ire. On the outside, our home looked normal now. No more smell or all that crying that my mom did. Just my dad's continuous cigar smoke filling the apartment. When I would ask him where he was going on the rare night he came home first he would tell me he was "going to see a man about a horse". I kept waiting and waiting and waiting for my horse to arrive but it never did. The truth was, he was going out with his girlfriend, the one he had me call "Aunt". He wasn't fooling me with that. She looked a lot like "Marilyn Monroe" in hair and skin coloring and body type. She took care of herself with perfume, powder, and pretty and alluring clothing. She had a daughter two years older than me and lived directly across the street from us. Her husband was what was called a "grouch" in those days. He was unpleasant to be around, unpleasant to everyone. I would say hello to him when he was around and he would just grunt at me and walk away. "Aunt DC" wasn't so bad to me. She actually tried to be helpful to me because she knew my mom was gone. In the summertime we would sit and play cards in her kitchen; me, her, and her daughter "BC". "BC" was decent to me even though she really was way too "in crowd" for me. "Aunt DC" let her run wild I thought. She came and went as she pleased, never had to say where she was going or what she was doing at 14. It should not have surprised me when "BC" showed up pregnant right after she graduated high school as she had already had two abortions and I guess she couldn't do it again.

But Aunt "DC" made sure she informed me I was dressing like a slut when I started high school. She asked me if I had a brush and powder set for my "other" hair and cheeks; I think you can understand what she was saying. I had on stockings and underwear and still the comment was made. I got really angry because for once I actually felt like I was one of the girls instead of a physically feeling less robot whose job was to be pushed around. This was the first year that I could wear regular clothes instead of school uniforms as well. I also was not so enamored with her when she was at our house one night in the living room with my father and he asked me to sit on his lap. After the incident with the nightgown I was not about to sit on his lap and when she asked me about it the next day I told her I felt like I might be molested by him if I sat on his lap; i.e. I was too old for that anymore. I guess it just didn't sit well with her that I never hugged or kissed my father and evidently she told him how she felt, thus, the request to sit on his lap. It wasn't that I gave it a lot of thought and decided not to hug or kiss him or sit on his lap. For that matter; I couldn't see any reason to do so.

"Aunt DC" died of cancer the summer before "BC" became pregnant. That was an awful time for me. It was all so veiled in secrecy that when they said she died I was shocked. I knew she was sick, I knew it was her liver, I knew she drank and smoked and took birth control pills and you shouldn't do that; but DIE!! I regretted that I ever got mad at her about what I should wear; she was just trying to protect me. Now it was too late. I was beside myself. I had gotten my first job as a waitress at age 15 at the diner in the little town we lived in and of course, the call about her dying came at 3 in the morning. If I was asleep when it came, I wasn't anymore. I got my uniform on and told my father I was going to work. He just grunted and rolled back over, no doubt drunk. Don't worry about his loss; he already had another girlfriend which eventually became his wife

10 years later. They waited until all their separate children were out of their respective homes before she moved in and they were married. She was a religious woman, so she demanded he marry her or no more sex. Needless to say, I absolutely hated her. I knew her also, just like I knew "DC" when she was my dad's current squeeze. This woman, "BH" was a chaperone in the extracurricular activity that my father was the director of and I was in the marching band with her 3 daughters. I saw a lot of her. Her girls absolutely loved my dad because their dad had died when they were very young and the youngest of them had no memory of her dad at all. So, they flocked to him. He was nice to them (he didn't have to live with them or be responsible for them so he could be nice). I guess in her own mind she was nice to us too, trying to pinch-hit for the mother we didn't have any more. One more time; my sister was the highly favored one. Quiet, unassuming, baby-like in behavior and looks, she was the much beloved one; and it was a blatant sympathy and partiality, you couldn't miss it. Not when she was young or now when she was older. She was a sneak and I was a bulldog. I did all the fighting for us and she reaped the benefits. If something went wrong it was my fault because I ***should have known better*** or because I was older; any excuse worked to take it out on me. Auntie also had chosen my sister as her favorite and because I got in the middle of an argument between Auntie and my sister (I took my sister's side) Auntie didn't talk to me for 17 years. Only after my sister passed on did Auntie begin talking to me again.

AIDS IN MY FAMILY

I hated it back then but now I am glad Auntie and my dad all treated my sister with favor because her life was suddenly cut short when she was only 34. She died of complications of AIDS; leaving behind her six year old daughter (who had been diagnosed with full blown AIDS at age two) and having had her 5 month old son die from complications of AIDS four years earlier. The best information at the time was that she had a 50/50 chance that each child could be born with AIDS. Not cumulative 50%, no, a new 50/50 for each pregnancy. She wound up with two that had the disease and this was the year before they found that they could give babies AZT to help prevent them from being born with AIDS. My sister only lived 8 years from her diagnosis, again, 1 year sooner than the cocktails that keep AIDS patients alive now were discovered. Thankfully, her daughter is now 21 and is expected to live a normal life span due to the new drugs that she responds to very well. She is now grown and engaged to be married.

That whole experience was a living hell for all of us. I had moved 1,200 miles away from everyone one year before she died and it was a cruel agony to live so far away at such a terrible, critical time of her life. The doctors weren't very helpful either. One week she was dying, the next she was better. Every day held the promise of "the drug" that would cure her so there was hope and then suddenly she was in a coma. Do we go visit her to say goodbye? What if we wait too long and she dies without my being able to tell her how much I loved her and how I will watch out for her daughter? What if my children don't see her alive and have to see her in her coffin? I had put down a prayer request on several prayer chains asking for God's perfect timing to go visit her so we could say goodbye. I even called the Christian radio station in my area and asked them to pray also. A short time after the radio station broadcast the request, my husband told me that his boss told him to go because he wasn't able to get any work done anyway and we left. When we arrived there my sister was in a coma. God brought her out of that coma just long enough for us to tell her how much we loved her. I don't believe she was aware that she was dying because the AIDS had attacked her brain and she had no short term memory. While I was there reading the Psalms to her when she slipped back into the coma she never came out of. I was facing the window which was across the bed from her. I hear a voice behind me saying don't leave your purse unattended and then she was gone. And so was my purse. We looked everywhere and it was gone. It happened that quickly. With my sister on her death bed, they stole my purse. I was alone, my husband took the kids skiing so I had to call him collect and ask him to call the credit card companies and our bank to freeze our accounts. Forget the money, my drugs were in there, license, keys, keepsakes from my sister, etc. etc. I was in a rage. Once again I felt that God let me down. Isn't he supposed to protect us as we are his special humans? (Psalm 32:7 – You are my hiding place; you will protect me from trouble and surround me with songs of deliverance. Psalm 37:28 – For the Lord loves the just and will not forsake His faithful ones they will be protected forever. Psalm 41:2-3 – The Lord will protect him and preserve his life, He will bless him in the land and not surrender him to the desire of his foes. The Lord will sustain him on his sickbed and restore him from his bed of illness.)

My kids were not in any way babies; my youngest was 10, the oldest 15. We were very candid with them about the fact that she was dying. We only told them on the way to say goodbye that she was dying and why; and they were mad. My oldest was furious at me for not telling her. My sister had me swear not to tell them EVER. It was a promise I felt I had to break out of my weakness. In and out of the hospital; one opportunistic disease to the next in her body, side effects from the medicine to kill the disease now was killing her; her child now without a mother to raise her.

Does history repeat itself? (My sister "lost" her mother at age 7; her daughter lost hers at age 6) I have to wonder. My sister's death gave my father a heart attack from which he almost died. He wound up having quadruple bypass surgery right after the funeral. It only bought him 7 more years of life because after that he died in 6 months of fighting a very aggressive throat cancer (remember all those cigars)? This meant more nightmares for me, sleepless nights, and now an antidepressant to remain able to function as a mother of 3 almost teenage children. During this same time things were really, really stressful for my husband at work, he really didn't need a grieving wife on top of that. But, despite our failings, God still loved us and brought us through that valley of death.

THE HIGH SCHOOL YEARS

The year when I needed to start high school, I told my father that I didn't want to go to any of the all-girls Catholic Academies. I wanted to attend public high school with all of the other kids in town. Since our town did not have its own high school we were provided transportation to get to another town's high school. I am thankful, I suppose that my sister had flunked out of catholic school and changed to public school; it gave me the break I needed to get out of that oppressive environment as well. Short of moving to another town to get away from the classmates I had been with for 9 years, this gave me a new environment where just about no one knew me. Most of my classmates went on to Catholic High School and the public school was so large that my chances of ever being in any class with any of those few students who knew me from grade school were slight. I could start over as a new person minus my grade school reputation.

All the freedom we were given in High School was frightening for me. I was now responsible to get the bus on time to get to the school in time for whatever class I was going to. I had to find my way through 3 floors of classrooms, some of which were ingeniously hidden between floors at the end of the hallway in the back of the school. I had only 5 minutes to get my stuff and get to my locker if I needed a book from it or to deposit some of my books instead of having to carry them everywhere all day long. There was no humiliation; at least not personal humiliation of a student by a teacher. Disciplinary action on students who didn't follow the rules and disrupt class, yes; they got sent to the Disciplinary Officer's room and were assigned detention or, if serious enough, suspended.

There was one teacher in Freshman Year, the last period of the day, who I had for General Science who had a propensity for talking very loudly and slapping a metal yardstick on empty desks which would jolt awake sleeping students in my class. I was scared of him and the other kids behaved, wouldn't you? But, for the most part, we were addressed as Miss Joan Public or Mr. John Public and were treated as though we had an IQ no higher than a monkey.

There was a new place in this school; something called homeroom. In grade school we didn't need homeroom, we were in the same classroom, same seat every day all day all year. Now, homeroom was at a certain time and everyone had to report to one at that time everyday, because that was when attendance for the record was taken. In all the other classes attendance was taken and matched against the homeroom tally and students were given "cut" slips if they were in homeroom and not in a later, or earlier, class that day. "Cuts" were given detention and if there were too many "cuts", a suspension would be given.

The reason I am going on and on about homeroom is because that is where I met my (future husband), "FH". The first day of school he was in my homeroom but I don't recall seeing him. The second day the teacher had the seating chart for our homeroom and it was alphabetical. My "FH's" last name began with the letter before mine in the alphabet so he sat directly in front of me. He began that first day of sitting in front of me to get me to go out with him. He didn't express his final objective, just began what later seemed like a well planned offensive to get me for himself. Of course, I ignored him steadfastly for quite a while. I had an awful lot to get used to as this school was definitely not the same as the one I had attended for 9 years.

But, it appeared that, "the gods" were conspiring against me by putting me next to this boy not only in homeroom but in study hall as well, twice a day. There he didn't even have to turn around to see me.

So, by sophomore year I was more at home at my new school and was telling my "FH" all about the boyfriends in my band or bands from out of town and telling him what we were doing. He always told me I deserved better than what these boys had to offer. They just wanted to use me for their pleasure; they didn't have any intention of treating me well.

He kept asking me WHY I wanted to be with guys who didn't respect me; guys who lied about what I did or didn't do, had girlfriends at home when they were not at competitions, had no plans of any future with me. I was way too sophisticated for this momma's boy, with the pimple faced, pepperoni pizza mug. I couldn't possibly think of him as anything but a guy who was obsessed with me with no chance of being with me. He had no involvement in any band activity. It wasn't his thing. He had been able to play a pretty decent trumpet in middle school but then he had surgery and was no longer able to play. It was a big disappointment to him.

Instead, he wrestled; moving from JV to Captain of JV to Varsity to eventually Captain of the Varsity Team in his senior year. I was persuaded to go to his wrestling matches. I wasn't particularly fond of wrestling; basketball was more my thing, but it took me out of my house at least one a week from Fall to Spring. Eventually I learned how to keep the book and how to run the clock and I did both. During that time I met some other guys that were involved with wrestling indirectly; one of which was our Valedictorian. "PL" was very Italian and very smart. I couldn't figure out why he was hanging out with these muscle heads, I'm sure he must have had something better to do!!! But, he continued to be there every match and I sat next to him in the stands to watch the matches. I couldn't imagine me; you know ME, sitting next to and being spoken to in a reasonable manner by our class Valedictorian. My extracurricular activities remained just that extracurricular – in another time and place.

"FH" had ridden the late bus home with me and walked me from the bus stop to my door. Sounds like I'm not exactly resisting him? He began to wear on me. He delivered the Sunday newspaper to our house and I saw him for a brief moment every Sunday morning before breakfast. He also "happened" to start liking the same professional baseball team that I did. That was another one of my dad's enjoyments. He took us to the stadium to see several of the games during my high school years and the games would always be on TV or radio so we could follow them. Being a girl and knowing the batting averages and pitching stats for all the players on that team challenged the boys in my homeroom as well as those who lived on "FH's" block. I would hang out at the corner with "the guys" and listen to the game with them. My team had always been an underdog and against all odds won the World Series that year.

By the time I was in 9th grade, my religiosity faded. I no longer went to mass and my father no longer pretended to care that I didn't. I threw out the baby with the bathwater at that point in time because it had just been too much. I now had them out of my face by going to a new location; would I be able to get them out of my mind as well? Evidently not.

I have been telling you about an extracurricular activity that I took part in from age 10 to 16 in various formats. I marched in a band. I played a fife at first but as I grew older, I carried a flag for a while, and then I learned how to twirl a rifle. This pursuit was fueled by my desire to be a winner and to spend time with my father who had also been in band, playing a base horn for 40 years, long before I was born.

As a matter of fact, in 1965 my father took my whole family with him to band competitions every Friday to Sunday all over the east coast. Some of the places were so far away that other people flew. We drove. Always drove. My mom loved car rides. So do I to this very day. So, each weekend we went to another stadium to watch my dad compete. We stayed in hotels, ate in restaurants, swam in pools, went to cookouts and lots and lots of parades. From St. Patty's Day to Veteran's Day there were parades my father participated in. By the time I was 10 I was marching in parades as well and continued to do so until I was 16. We belonged to different bands and so the parades we marched in were different. If there was a conflict my dad would skip his. He had always wanted to march in the Macy's Thanksgiving Day Parade and a few years before he passed away he did. We taped it off the TV so we have it today. It was one of the highlights of his life. And I was very blessed to have this remembrance when he suddenly died of cancer (they had given him two years and he died after only 6 months! So it was suddenly).

So, the big contest that year was in Washington, DC. ALL the big, good bands were there to compete and so was my dad's band. Funny the things you remember, but my father was driving our station wagon when he ran out of gas on the Potomac River Drawbridge at 1 a.m. in the morning. We kids thought it was a blast. Auntie and her cousin "NW" were not having a blast. We had to get out of the car on the bridge and wait for a tow truck. There were no gas stations nearby and no bathrooms either. I remember the wind blowing on that bridge. It sure makes a person have to pee. Thankfully one of my dad's band members recognized our car and took my dad to get gas and we eventually got off that bridge. For a long, long time I had a fear of bridges and heights. I wonder if that was where that came from.

My dad's band won that big important contest that year. It was the achievement of a lifetime. I don't believe they ever won that title again! My little band that was in the town I lived in wasn't that highly ranked. We were usually 4th out of 6 bands competing, but that left plenty of room for improvement and practice we did.

COLOR GUARD

My big success was with the color guard of that band. We had our own competition season in January and had our own routine that we all had to memorize. We were ok the first year but then my dad hired "FK", a drill instructor well known in the circuit we competed in as top notch. And if you could survive his training and still compete, you did win, and win consistently. And so we did, contest after contest, season after season. Because "FK" lived 2+ hours away from our town my father offered him a place to sleep in our house. It was me, my sister and my dad. I had a combination of fear and awe for "FK". I wanted him to like me so badly. I wasn't the best rifle and the judges consistently wrote down "rifle with glasses" on the drill score sheets to compute our score so much that "FK" told me I had to march from then on without the glasses so they couldn't follow me and my mistakes which cost us points in the final score. I didn't think anything of his staying with us in our house on Friday and Saturday nights until I was standing at the sink doing some dishes on a

Saturday morning before a competition and he came up behind me and began feeling me up. Terror sprang up in me. "What do I do?" If he persists I am going to have to do what he wants or he will disgrace me in front of the band members every single practice and God only knows what he will tell my father; that I approached *him* for sex? As he nuzzled my neck I pushed his hands down and off me, evidently he understood that I wasn't volunteering to service him. I never told anyone about what happened, I couldn't. No one would believe me anyway. I have an 8 x 10 black and white photo of us with trophies as tall as we were, for the three years we competed under that drill instructor. We all had big smiles on our faces but I still wonder today (long after he had died), if he was successful in molesting any of the other girls in the color guard.

In freshman year I had a class that I had never heard of before but was very informative, it was called Health. If I could give it a title I guess I would call it the "instruction manual for your physical body class". Indeed, I learned a lot in that class. I learned that we had a brain inside our skull and that there could possibly be differences between the way people do things and it was okay. It wasn't until 5 years later that I discovered the book "I'm Ok, You're Ok". I read the book and took the course based on it from the local community college and it was very helpful to my young, naïve, and narrow, way of thinking. I was in a strait jacket of beliefs that were no longer helpful to my life. It was from there that I researched and found my first Psychiatrist; one of the ones that had treated my mother. I don't even know how I got his name or knew he had treated my mother. There was public transportation available to get there; in fact, it was on the way to my father's business. I know that after a while I stopped seeing him because it looked like he slept through my appointments. He certainly never had any advice for me. I didn't tell my father I was seeing a psychiatrist, no less one of the ones that treated my mother. The Dr. charged me a small amount of money for the visits because of my age and ability to pay, I think. Maybe there was no discount but because I had so few expenses the fee didn't seem exorbitant to me. He certainly never had any comments for me. I guess it still did some good in helping me understand the world I lived in and what my dysfunctional family really was all about.

By sophomore year I also began to look to certain teachers for wisdom and other things; one of which was to answer the questions I didn't bother to broach with my father or auntie. I was so used to being shook off when I tried to talk that I just gave up. I admired my Spanish teacher who walked with a brace on her leg from having contracted Polio as a child (before Jonas Salk made a vaccine to stop it). I also gravitated to my Biology teacher who was a man whose wife taught freshman English (I didn't have her). I was so proud to show him my birth control pills. My "FH" was in this class with me and the teacher knew we were going out. He said that I was being very responsible. That if I felt I was ready for sex I needed to take care of myself. I guess being a man he knew what men do with women. I would NEVER have imagined that his advice would prove true. I still send this teacher a Christmas card every year; oops, I forgot he was Jewish. Yikes!!! I guess it IS the ***thought*** that counts.

I was very attracted to my Psychology Teacher for different reasons than the ones listed above. He treated me like I was a genius in class, and I didn't know that he could see my neediness like a bull can see a red cape. So, it came to the point where he and I had met outside of school and we were in his car doing heavy petting. He would not go further (he knew he could either get arrested or lose his job or both, I suspect). He referred me to his friend who would be more than happy to help me out. So, "AX" and I met at a hotel and "did the nasty". I can't remember if I ever met him for sex again. I felt nothing, no physical sensation, no emotional connection, so what was the point? I had not felt anything with the Army Recruiter, or the "college student" I had sex with and very limited sensations with the Psychology Teacher. I was humiliated by then because I thought I knew what I should have looked and sounded like to the man I was having sex with and I just couldn't meet those expectations. I felt defective and dirty as usual. I found out later that I could have done everything except penetration and still be a "virgin". I could have avoided all those years of guilt and shame by doing that. Where was President Clinton when I needed him?

UNC AND THE STORE

By the time I was 16, I was employed in the business that my father and auntie owned. I would take the bus from the town where school was for a short distance and then switch busses so that I finally got to where I needed to be. I did my homework on the busses. I felt so grown up I didn't mind the cold, rain, snow, heat, etc, etc. that I encountered taking the busses. I had a job!!! I worked every weekday from after school to closing. Some nights my father closed; others, Unc closed. On the nights that Unc closed we used to talk. It became talk, and talk, and talk. It was some out of boredom and some out of concern for me. My unc knew that I was no stranger to boys and he didn't want to see me get hurt. His daughter was 10 years younger than me so this would be good practice for him I thought. I felt special because no one gave me positive attention like this. We would go up the road to the Chinese Restaurant every so often and eat after we closed the store. I had never eaten Chinese food, my dad was a steak and potatoes man and it was steak and potatoes and not much else.

Not even PIZZA. I had never even heard of anyone who did not like pizza, but if it wasn't a steak... Anyway, I digress. In the summer when it didn't get dark until 9 pm or later we would go for car rides after we closed the store. Unc took me on roads I didn't even know existed. Single lane winding roads down close to the river, we went from town to town to town. Some towns were only blocks long but the ride was always long following the river. Sometimes we would stop and park the car and take a break. Still talking, by the way. The net result was that Unc knew every detail of my non-existent sex life. At least at the beginning it was non-existent. As time went on I became more and more curious what this was all about. He used to call me a "Zophtic" woman that would make good babies. Oh, wonderful, a sex machine with good reproductive prospects. Was that all I was good for? Even so, I guess I should have been thankful that anyone saw me as being useful for anything even sex.

The TV, movies, magazines, other teens, and adults at the diner where I also worked said sex was great. But, my father's friend's daughter got knocked up the beginning of sophomore year and disappeared out of my geometry class in the spring. Maybe that was why my father, when he saw me walking with a boy at one of the summer competitions away from the stadium and toward a wooded private area, started screaming at me to come back over to where he was standing. Here is this guy who doesn't really care about what I do as long as he can enjoy himself, screaming at me for walking with a boy toward a

wooded area?! I, of course, was completely humiliated because this boy was a few years older than me
and I'm sure he was also embarrassed that the girl he
was with was being told she had to go with her daddy
into the stadium instead of with him into the woods
where we could have some privacy. I **liked** this boy.
He acted nice to me, acted like he cared for me and
my father had to ruin the whole thing. Needless to
say, I had it out with my father but, just like all the
other times, he didn't care what I was feeling or
needed; he called me a slut and insisted that I stay
with him the rest of the day; at least he didn't slap me
across the face this time.

Shortly thereafter, I found an assortment of
condoms under my "friend" the radio on my night-
stand. I WASN'T DOING ANYTHING THAT I
NEEDED THEM FOR!!!!! I was **hot**. Not the kind
of hot you're thinking, silly. Hot as in enraged. I am
NOT that type of girl, I do not do that, I had promised not to do that and had struggled against my
own curiosity. I had seen the parish priest with my
dilemma and he told me that boys could use a pipe
just as efficiently as me to attain their satisfaction.
Sex was for marriage and marriage only. Remember
before you laugh that this was the 70's; the free love
revolution you know: free love, love the one you're
with, etc, etc. This was no easy commitment. And
finding those condoms there was so humiliating to
me. I wasn't strong enough morally to stand up for
what I believed in and for that my child was killed.
I also hated myself and fulfilled the requirements to
be hated by my woman hating father. Another man

("FH") having to put up with being limited or turned down when requesting sex because of my earlier scarring. There was no love here, just taking, taking, taking. I felt violated. By age 16, I would have had to be dead not to know that. We were all broads to my father, or worse yet b*****s, including me. Not my sister, but me. My father told my "FH" that he was getting the short end of the stick if he married me. My father liked my "FH" very much and I was glad for that as my husband's dad was on the road most of the time and therefore he spent very little time with him.

For me to see that my dad treated me just like a whore (which is what he felt we were only good for) really hurt. I felt violated, and dirty, but that was his problem. In his own inept way he was trying to…I was going to say protect me, but hello, he was trying not to have the problems his friend had with his daughter turning up pregnant at 16 and they did NOT believe in abortion. Besides, that was the last year abortion was still illegal so the parents could not force her to have one. She had the child, a son by that "boy" who exposed himself to me previously and laughed as I ran off.

By the time I had my own children I could understand why he acted like he did; but at the time he threw my world into chaos and I broke out in shingles on my right breast around to my back along the nerve. I didn't know what it was, I just knew something was itching like mad and burned like crazy. I wasn't about to show my dad and I didn't like to have to show my auntie; but those were the two choices I was given. I didn't drive yet and didn't want to go to the general practitioner that I could walk to so I chose Auntie. She didn't tell me but she had her suspicion of what it was and she took me directly to a dermatologist and I had to let her watch the doctor examine me. He confirmed the diagnosis of shingles. (Shingles are caused by stress. They were a reactivation of the chicken pox virus that I had contracted in childhood. Supposedly only adults get shingles.) I wanted to die, I felt so ashamed, especially when auntie said "**What in the world** does a 16 year old have to be worried about"? How about whether or not to violate my conscience and my religion by sleeping with my very insistent boyfriend? I think that qualified. I never told her that was it, I just played dumb. Her husband, on the other hand, knew exactly, blow by blow what I was going through on the question of giving in to a very insistent boyfriend. "FH" was the first and only male I had ever met who cared about something OTHER than sex. And, we had known each other for two years and been going out steady for a period of time in the previous year. Some might say that he was very patient with me to have waited that long. He saw how smart I was and how pretty. He took me home to meet his family. Yes, a *family* consisting of a mother and father, older brother, younger brother, younger sister and grandmother, all living in the same house; The Cleavers, the Wards, the Reeds, the Beverly Hillbillies'; only kidding. But they looked like that which in reality didn't exist; the perfect family, but I didn't know that at the time. He also saw how my father treated me. When he was around, my father was nicer to me so that he wouldn't lose face to my "FH". HE WAS my knight in shining armor, come to rescue me from the evil ones. But, if I did have sex with him, I was going to hell. Forget even about the possibility of my getting pregnant, I was too smart for that. I understood exactly when and how that happens and I went and got fitted for a diaphragm because I couldn't tolerate hormonal methods. That was taken care of; one less thing to have to worry about. Until I turned up pregnant 3 weeks before the wedding (you have to put the diaphragm IN for it to prevent pregnancy). I hadn't put it in because I thought it was too late in my cycle to get pregnant and I wasn't planning on having sex away from home.

By the time I finally gave him what he wanted I was glad that my father really liked "FH" because many a night my father would come home to a red-faced daughter, sweating and trying to hide the physical evidence of that which I somehow managed to justify. It wasn't "all the way" so I didn't violate the "rules". Nonetheless, I was so humiliated. I still couldn't believe my father put those condoms under my radio and now, here I am, confirming the correctness of his action. This created an intolerable conflict within me, which caused me to split off several alter personalities to handle the conflicts.

It became a conflict I could not abide and after graduation from High School I broke it off with "FH". I told him I simply could not continue to sin like that. I believed he really cared about me but that wasn't enough. During that time I slept with a man who frequented my father's business, the college student, just once, to "prove" I was desirable. I was trying to show "FH" that I was worth "the struggle" to do what I asked and wait until we were married to have sex (marry me ___now___), but I never told him I slept with the college student so I guess I really was the one who needed the reassurance. I was so humiliated and yet I acted like the cool, cosmopolitan, well-educated woman that I thought I needed to be. The only person who believed *that* was me. I didn't have the knowledge or experience to know that the man I slept with knew what the real thing was supposed to be like and I wasn't doing that!!!! I suspect it was the same for the Military Recruiter I slept with. My "FH" and I tried to enlist in the Military believing we could see the world, get educated, and escape from my father. Oops. Did I say that? Of course, none of the attention that this Recruiter gave me swayed my desire or opinion in any way. Duh. I was so naïve. Both my "FH" and I failed the admission physical; His for color blindness which would never change, and me for a kidney condition that I have never again tested positive for. I believe God protected us from a terrible future in the Military. We were both too wounded emotionally to have survived what we were trying to do. And, the whole idea that we would be stationed together as they promised; even a child could tell you that wasn't going to happen.

After being rejected by the Military, I attended secretarial school in the big city, but not for long. I had excelled in everything at the school in the big city except human relationships 101. Three of the girls who were in my High School Class also went to this school in the big city. I knew of the girls but never really had any interaction with any of them. One of their older sisters marched in my band and one of the girls herself was a flag twirler in our high school which gave her "in crowd" status. One of the three was FAT, not my imagination but FAT, and had been all through high school. Her older brother was morbidly obese and the subject of ridicule at school. He graduated before we began classes there. It was a single mother family, their father had died many years earlier and back then it really put the mother in a bind to support all 3 of her children on the meager salary she could earn even as a nurse.

Since we had to take the same public transportation to get to the school, it gave them opportunity to torment me. I was so relieved to be out of high school and out into the real world where people treat you decently that it really threw me for a loop when those girls made their appearance and started to mock me and turn the other students against me. I had wanted to make a friend here among all the new people from all the different parts of the city. I even had my hair professionally colored something very different from what I had had, and cut. I bought new "mod" glasses (since I decided I needed to be able to actually see the class work) lost some weight and picked out some new "with it" clothes. These changes only made it worse. There was no guidance counselor to run to so I asked the dean of students if I could transfer to the branch of the school in my state, away from the big city and those girls. The answer was yes and my father allowed me to drive my new car there each day. It was at least 30 minutes of Highway driving each way, but I had peace with the humans. The teachers were something else. Their counterpart school in the big city had all brand new equipment and I could not make the transition to the old equipment at the school I transferred to, and the teachers just didn't want to hear my excuses.

My first job in the big city was at the World Headquarters of a major hotel chain. Each day at lunch I would go walking and exploring, shopping. There was so much to see and do and I wanted to do it all right then. I felt a freedom like I had never known before. Now I only had one boss and she was very nice to me. I would pass by my father if we both happened to be in the same place at the same time but that didn't occur very often. Since my "FH" and I had broken up, I began meeting a man who also worked in the city but lived in the suburbs. He was quite a bit older than me and I felt like if I continued to let him buy me lunch every day I would have to "repay" him with sex and I wasn't interested. We stopped having lunch. Meanwhile, I was very interested in what "FH" was up to now that he was free. He was working for my father in several capacities; at the shop with the bleach and ammonia and at the business that my father had just bought. He was also going to college full time during the day. One day on the way to college he fell asleep at the wheel and scraped the divider on the major highway that he had to take and the next day he quit college. He wanted to live and it was obvious he couldn't do all that was expected of him.

Somehow in the midst of this life changing event another reshuffling of priorities took place and he asked me to marry him. When he told his parents, his father said he was an *******. How's that for support?

I was shocked and happy at the same time; his asking me to marry him told me that I was a worthwhile person, an attractive and smart woman, someone very important. It's too bad that that revelation didn't take place until later after we had separated and I was living with a friend temporarily. But, for today it was so exciting. My "FH" came from that "cleaveresque" family above but there was a lot going on that I could not see this early in my relationship with them. One of those things was their financial situation and the system under which money decisions were made. "FH"'s father drove a truck over the road in order to provide for all those kids and wife and only came home on weekends. He was very tired when he got home and he didn't spend very much time with my "FH". Also, since "FH's" mother didn't work outside the home (I wonder where she could have put THAT in her schedule!), and truck driving didn't give them a large amount of disposable income, things were tight. Money was scarce. "FH's" mother was trained by HER mother how to recycle everything but toilet paper because they had lived through the great depression and the only way there was food on the table was by what they could grow in the yard and hunt in the woods. They bathed once a week just like in the "Little House on the Prairie" days. They saved water and sewer by not flushing every time someone used the toilet. The whole point to this part of my dissertation is that my "FH" had started working as a paper boy when he was 10 and he saved every penny he earned for 7 years to buy me not just ANY ring, but a one carat marquis cut diamond. My unc's friend had connections and was able to get a much larger stone than "FH" could afford. I sure had all the physical trappings of a future bride and wife. I had a beautiful wedding gown (not the one I wanted but the one I could afford, had blue ribbon on it in the neckline, sleeves and veil and an empire waist that would not show the bloating from the pregnancy). I had had a huge engagement party and bridal shower. One thing our parents had (on both sides) were relatives and friends whose kids were older and were given to by our parents, so we wound up really well. Then there was the cash from the wedding. Amazing. I was really blessed, I just didn't know it.

After the wedding I discovered how my mother-in-law really felt about me. She nicknamed me "glooper". Believe me, "glooper" was not a positive moniker. I earned that title by not knowing how to do basic wifely functions such as cooking a turkey without taking the insides out, putting a top crust on a pumpkin pie and I don't even remember what else. Not having had a mother, I was at a loss for the information that most new brides would have had back when we were first married. Forget about her giving me a see-through green baby doll for my birthday a year before we were getting married. I don't know

WHAT she was thinking; there is nothing I can speculate that would have made this acceptable. But I wound up being called "glooper". This name was used by her and the other relatives at every family gathering for birthdays and holidays. In frustration I named my first puppy "glooper". The puppy was not something I planned; it wound up being a birthday present from my husband. It was a hunting breed, small size, and I, never having had a pet other than a bird or a fish, wanted to try it. I was hoping it would be ok in our little apartment, but it wasn't.

MORE SEXPLOITATION

Despite all the good things during the time period before the wedding, I began to feel very tired and couldn't understand why. It was months before I wound up pregnant before the wedding. There was a new doctor in town so I went to him. I was an adult now; a physically mature one who wasn't comfortable with any doctor who knew about my previous bad behavior and my mother's situation.

So, I tried this new doctor. He was young, maybe early thirties. Good looking, drove a motorcycle. His waiting room was filled every time I went there. He did some blood work and a physical exam which required me to put on a hospital type gown. He listened to my lungs, checked my reflexes, looked in my eyes and throat and said that I needed B-12 injections, once a week. He said that was why I was so tired. I told him that Bebop had pernicious anemia and he said that was why I was anemic too. Back then I didn't know that pernicious anemia was caused by a defect in the bone marrow which makes red blood cells and I didn't have that condition. If anything, I just slipped back into excessive blood loss anemia from heavy periods and not eating enough iron. Whatever. So, I started coming weekly and those shots burned. They were given in the gluteus but first I had to have a physical before he could give me the shot. So, off came the clothes and on went the gown. Those physicals were weird though; he had me stand up facing the narrow edge of the exam table and lean into the table with my legs spread. He then had me do a stationary walk during which time he listened to my heart. He told me he had to do this because I had an enlarged heart. Also not true I found out later from a reputable doctor. Listening to my heart wasn't the only thing he was doing. I didn't think an enlarged heart gave him cause for him to fondle and abuse my genitals. After I don't know HOW MANY weekly visits, the nurse came in while he was doing one of his physicals on me and the doctor had a fit. Next time I came she was gone. He knew what he was doing was wrong and somehow I found out that that waiting room was crowded because he was doing this to all the young, tight bodied 20 year olds. He finally just asked me to have sex with him and I declined and stopped going there. It left me scarred. Maybe 10 years later I heard that he had died in a motor-cycle crash. Maybe there is some kind of justice in the universe after all.

"In the Universe?" Where did that come from? Since I had stopped going to church I began looking for answers to why I was here. Why I was born when I was the victim of so much neglect and abuse? What was I supposed to be doing? Is there an afterlife? Is there only one way to get there? Can anyone be absolutely sure they are going there? I figured only the "Saints" of the Church (not the New Orleans Saints football team) were up there with God because Jesus was still on the cross at least part of everyday in the masses that took place.

The wedding was now months away, and after I actually was surprised by that wedding shower, I had all this stuff that needed to go somewhere. The month of the wedding we rented our first apartment, that gave us 3 weeks to get everything set up, get the furniture delivered in addition to putting all the stuff from the shower and whatever personal belongings that we didn't need on a daily basis. We had spent quite a bit of time looking for an apartment. My "FH" didn't want to spend above "X$" a month in rent and that amount put us in a poor neighborhood about 15 minutes from the town we grew up in. It was a third floor walk up above a retail establishment. The Landlord lived on the 2nd floor. Drug addicts used the overhang of the building entrance for shelter and got stoned after purchasing their drugs across the street in the park. On the other corner was a bar. And, after my "FH" quit college, the only job he could get was Midnights, so that left me all alone with *that* outside all night, most nights. I was scared silly and not happy. I was also working and we could have afforded a more expensive apartment but "FH" always knew I could turn up pregnant at any time and there goes the income to pay that higher rent. I tried to make the best of it because it was OUR home. OUR home where everything would be perfect;

perfect because I was finally away from my psycho dad and over-invested Unc and my least favored daughter & niece status being shoved in my face on a routine basis. I didn't have to listen to the fights between my father and Auntie or Unc or between my cousins downstairs. I didn't have to be an unwilling participant in all the issues around that house. There was a lot of fighting going on everywhere. *Our* home was where the sisters have no place, neither did the priest who cancelled his part of our wedding, hours before the ceremony because of an "emergency" and didn't even have the courtesy to call my house, no, he called Auntie and told her. Coward. That's ok because that was what it took for me to walk out of that cult like church. I'd rather go to hell, thank you, than live under their rules and hypocritical clergy. So, after we came home from the honeymoon, we began attending my now husband's church.

THE ABORTION

I immediately availed myself of that Pastor's supposed influence over my husband as he had been going there for years. I asked him to talk to him and tell him not to force me to have that abortion. He said he would not because my new husband had not come in to talk to him. It would not be proper to break a confidence and confront him; and my new husband was NOT about to go talk to him about this. (As much as I hated the Church I grew up in, the leader **was** steadfastly pro-life). How was what that Pastor was saying the truth? The good news the Pastor gave me was that no matter what sin I committed, it was forgiven. God has *already* forgiven me for the abortion, I needed to lighten up. Lighten up indeed as I was vomiting all day and night long and trying to conceal the emotional chaos and disaster going on inside as I murdered my child because I was a coward. One of the reasons I hated my father so much was because he was a coward. He climbed into the bottle and left us CHILDREN not only to care for ourselves but my mom as well.

It proved to be an interesting honeymoon trying to ignore the "elephant in the living room" of my pregnant state and my pleading with my husband to have the child. I could not have sex with him on the honeymoon; sex is what caused me to wind up in the mess I was in. He was furious with me. He said I could have the child but he would be gone. How could I support a child when I couldn't even support myself? There were no pregnancy centers to help women back then. It was the year after abortion became legal in the state in which I lived. After I left my husband a few months later I asked my father if I could come home and he said no, that I had made my bed now I could sleep in it. I hadn't even approached him with the abortion/baby and the answer was NO! But my sister was allowed to move back home after her marriage fell apart when she learned her then husband was a liar and really didn't want children like she did. She was so naïve that she didn't even know the basic mechanics of sex and why she wasn't getting pregnant. To his credit my father didn't let her back upstairs in his apartment but had Auntie clear a space in the basement and she used the bathroom upstairs for showers.

The honeymoon was finally over (one week long) and we were home. My new husband went back to work the next day and I had my "Aunt" DC's daughter "BC" (remember her from the previous chapter?) take me to the doctor for the abortion. There was no sedative, no anesthesia, just a painful shot into the cervix and the sucking sound of the vacuum machine. I had terrible cramps and pain but it was over *fairly* quickly. I was crying and the nurse there tried to tell me that it wasn't a baby, it was just the "products of conception" but I knew better. I was a murderer.

They told me to get up and go out to the desk and pay for the procedure and then go home. That was it. Nothing for pain, nothing to erase that horrific sound and my imagination's rendering of what I did to that child, NOTHING!!!!! And I wasn't going to have it so I lay down on the floor below the window where you pay and closed my eyes. Another patient came out to pay and saw me there and screamed. All of a sudden I had lots of attention. I could have done without the ammonia salts up my nose, however. They took me back to the back to rest some more. Of course this all backfired as my "girlfriend" "Aunt" "BC's" daughter left a message with the receptionist that she had to leave and I could find my own way home to the apartment. I wound up calling my mother in law. No, it wasn't all that bad. She knew about the pregnancy because I got sick at her house when we were visiting and she was frying bologna for her husband. She said to me as I came out of the bathroom "You're acting like you're pregnant"! I matter of factly told her I was and without any registering of concern, shock or surprise she said "are you keeping it?" I told her I wasn't and she said "Then don't talk about it". I could see where my husband got his belief system from; there was no sanctity of life in that home. Maybe it is genetic because I cannot understand how any grandmother could say something like that about her future grandchild. I am now a grandmother and even though I didn't want to be a grandmother when my first grandchild was conceived, I begged my daughter not to kill him, but to give him life. And she did. He drowned two years later but we all tried to do the right thing for him in his short little life. I was so proud of my daughter. The same thing happened with my son and they did not abort my beautiful grandgirl even though he had no marketable skills and was only 19 at the time. The Lord richly blessed them for choosing life.

After the abortion, I was suicidal. I felt that killing myself would be a good payment for killing my baby. We had decided to wait until after the honeymoon to have the abortion, I was hoping to talk him out of the abortion during the honeymoon when there was less pressure on him. I was 10 weeks along when I had it. While I was praying and begging and fuming and threatening my "FH", I was working in a new job in another part of the big city. I was so upset I ran my mouth to anyone who would listen. I received a lot of negative feedback even though I was portraying myself as self assured and liberated and able to take care of my "problem" myself.

One person was kind to me. He was a supervisor on another floor of the company I worked for and I had to bring memos to him twice a day every day. I wound up breaking down on him and an emotional affair began. I actually had a reason to live; I looked forward to waking up each morning. I couldn't wait to get to work. Little did I know I was so desperate for love; forget love, I needed kindness, esteem, forgiveness, a way out of my mess. He told me it wasn't a good idea to be broadcasting to anyone in the company that would listen that I was pregnant and going to have an abortion the day after the honeymoon. I didn't listen, hence that negative feedback I mentioned above!! I never said I didn't deserve my comeuppance. He told me I didn't need to have the abortion but had no solution for the money it would take to raise a child or where I could live to raise the child I didn't have to abort. He was 10 years older than me. He had two children, one of which was still an infant. His wife was having an affair on him and he was heartbroken. He wanted to leave her but couldn't even "THINK" about leaving his two boys. I guess that was why he was trying to convince me not to abort my child. I did it as I said and was then suicidal. I was, however, still a coward; so I couldn't pull the suicide off. So I thought. Later on I discovered that God kept me from suicide then and again 20 years later. I got to live and be miserable. As I said, my husband and I separated and I left the apartment to him and took my clothes to stay at a friends. I couldn't stay there forever, her husband wanted me gone and I still didn't have enough money for my own place (though I could have gotten it eventually). The biggest factor was that Mr. X said that he couldn't leave his kids so he was going to stay and duke it out with his wife. This was after I had had sex with him; actually, that is a very charitable description of what we had; I was able to feel loved emotionally and physically to a point and then shut down. It didn't help that I broke out laughing. He thought that I was insulting his member, which was the smallest on the face of the earth, I swear. I watched porno and read Playgirl so I knew what size it should have been by then. I was devastated but I went back to the apartment and told my husband that if he wanted me back he would have to go to counseling with me because I couldn't live that way. I was eaten up with guilt, shame, hopelessness and much more. He said who would I want to counsel us? I said I would call our "so forgiving" Pastor and ask him if he could do it. He could not, but he gave me the name of the denomination's "family services" branch where trained counselors helped religious people on a sliding scale based on income. I thanked him and made the call. I was able to get an appointment with a man who I thought said he was an Episcopal Priest. Not our denomination but I knew enough about what they called Episcopal in the states and Anglican in England. I couldn't wait for our first appointment.

When we arrived he looked "priestly enough" with a huge wooden cross that reached down to almost his belly button over a typical protestant minister shirt (I can't remember if he had a white collar or not, it didn't matter to me). He asked us why we were there and my husband's answer was "because she won't have sex with me". I guess I wasn't expecting him to say that immediately before I could get my mouth open (quite a feat that he did for those of you who know me already). The "priest" didn't miss a beat and asked me if I masturbated. If I could have melted down into a puddle that then seeped through the floor and out into the street I would have. I don't know, boy, these *clergy* sure don't act like what I thought clergy should act like. First the abortion forgiving minister, now this priest asking about masturbation.

I gave him the answer and we had an hour and a half long discussion, during which I learned that this "Priest" flew the coop. He was no longer a practicing priest. I asked him if he was married and he said no, so that wasn't the typical answer I was expecting. He said that the kind of problems we/I were having were going to take both individual and group sessions. Group every week and husband alone the other week and wife alone on the off week. I was relieved and afraid at the same time. I was afraid of the group, and glad to get a chance to see the counselor alone without my husband so I could give my side of the story.

Remember, this wasn't my first counselor. I tried that psychiatrist who was a waste of time (unless I wanted medication which I didn't). Then there was the "helpful" Psychology teacher. He referred me to his friend for sex and to a psychologist in another town. I think I saw him all of twice. I think I stopped seeing anyone at all because I was thinking that marriage was going to solve all my problems. I found out the hard way that you bring your problems with you into the marriage and so does your spouse so now you have to deal not only with the familiar dysfunction but the new dysfunction that the spouse brings into the marriage. I couldn't shut down the voices in my head reminding me constantly of how evil I was, how God saw what I did to my baby and how I was going to burn a good long time in purgatory if not permanently in hell for it.

That's ok. The question that "priest" asked wasn't even the most bizarre question I found myself answering about sex. My father liked my new husband so much that he took him to strip bars after work; and for a special treat my father invited us over for Sunday afternoon Porno flicks. His wife was supposedly saved and she let this stuff in their house? I found out that my father "needed" it to get him "in the mood" so she said. I was so humiliated that after a couple of times I just said I couldn't go there anymore but thanks for thinking of us. Once again I felt dirty, violated, and ashamed; and it became the only way I could feel anything physically with my husband. I hated that but I had to find a way to give him what he needed. We tried alcohol to try and get my mind to let go and allow me to feel, without success. I think it made things worse. So did trying to have sex with me while I was asleep and pinching my butt in or copping a feel in public. My new husband was informed that that behavior was inappropriate and it needed to stop. He did. I was afraid he was going to hit me like he did while we were going out. I had told him at that time that I would not tolerate him hitting me ever again and at that point we weren't married yet so I could have called it off had he not changed his behavior. He did stop; he simply became more skilled at controlling, insulting, and mocking; all behaviors the males in his life demonstrated for him with their own wives/women in their lives. Lest you think I was blameless in the relationship, I hit him back that day. I had to promise to never do that again and I did promise and never did it again.

Even though we were back living together, it took time before the counseling began to work to bring peace in our relationship. I, however, still had a tremendous need for love and raging hormones all at once. I pursued a man at work on my own floor; as a matter of fact he worked about 10 feet from me. I was informed that in addition to his being married and his wife being pregnant again that he was having an affair with a married woman next door who eventually wound up pregnant I hope with her husband's child. I did not like being told NO. So, one day an African American man asked me to have a drink with him after work and I was so stupid that even though it didn't feel right, I was a liberated woman and so I accepted. It didn't take him more than 10 minutes to ask me to sleep with him. The man that rejected me referred me to this man who was more than happy to try and help out. I'm sure his wife wouldn't agree. I told him no and he asked if it was because he was black. I told him that wasn't it that I just wasn't going to have sex with people from work anymore.

We wound up moving too far to commute into the city for work so I switched jobs to something closer and gave up looking for sex at work. I was introduced to marijuana at the new job as a gift for my birthday. We went out to eat, the switchboard operator and me, and for desert she lit up a joint and then offered me some. I found myself so lonely and needy at this point that even though I knew it was wrong, I did it. It helped the loneliness and shame from the abortion go away for a little while. Of course, I took it home and introduced my husband to it. It wasn't the answer for my problem or his but it was a while before we found the answer we needed and the pot seemed to help pass the time.

I'm OK, You're OK

Since the clergy had struck out trying to help us, I began reading self-help books. I read and took a course on Thomas Harris' "I'm Ok, you're Ok", and since I had a long bus/train commute every day to work I had a lot of time to read. Next up was the book "Positive Thinking" by Dr. Norman Vincent Peale. I soaked up his books and put them into practice. I felt better about myself. I was now in group counseling and that actually was wonderful. I learned so much about why I was so screwed up. I learned all about Adult Children of Alcoholics and how Alcoholics produce crazy thinking by continuously and unfailingly telling the non-alcoholic family members that whatever it is they are saying or thinking is incorrect. This was like being programmed or brainwashed. With the right kind of individual it is very successful in getting the Alcoholic everything he wants at everyone else's expense without any consequences for himself. My husband had me convinced *I was* crazy. Only through the groups' positive feedback about reality and the counselor's direction did I know where to start looking for change.

And, of course, when one person in a family system changes, the others are forced to change. Not forced like with a gun to their heads, forced like I'm not behaving that way anymore or I'm not accepting that ridiculous behavior anymore. Either they change or they lose the relationship. What I am describing was the very tip of the iceberg of deprogramming all that garbage that the priests, sisters, their helpers and my family did to me.

I had a great deal of rage, and the counselor told us to beat mattresses which he supplied at our counseling sessions with our fists and scream to get it out. We used to role play with the people we couldn't say the things that we needed to say to them. But we had to take turns being both people which helped us to think about what might have been going on in them or what had happened to them to have them respond the way they did. The premise was that if you have enough information you can change behavior. Indeed this was not going to be the last time I had cognitive thinking treatment for my pain. And every time I had a new therapist, psychologist, psychoanalyst, minister, alcoholic family systems therapist, or marriage counselor, I learned something useful; but the same problems kept popping up in response to things I KNEW I had resolved. We wound up leaving this group when the leader suggested that I sleep with one of the other women's husband who was like a father figure in age and wisdom. Too bad his wife didn't see it that way. She went up one side of me and down the other even though my husband had given his permission to me to do "the nasty" with her husband. He was pretty desperate to have sex himself since I wasn't able to give him what he needed.

Also, I had had my first child and apparently she disturbed the group meeting just by existing. The group members voted and my baby was banned from the group meetings, but I was still seeing the "priest" individually. Because of the long distance between our home and the meeting place I inevitably had to nurse my baby during our sessions. At one point the priest asked me to show him my breasts since they were exposed somewhat for nursing. I thought it might help so I did. All the priest counselor did was look and tell me how pretty they were. He was in no way threatening. Upon further evaluation I don't think it helped much! Because of these events I knew it was over. I felt really stupid for trusting that counselor but up to that point we had done a lot of good work both alone and in the group with others and it made me feel good to accomplish something and to be validated that I wasn't crazy, the family where I grew up was. And I was actually beginning to develop friendships with the members. We exchanged phone numbers and last names and got together outside the group setting. I had never really had a friend so this was exciting. We didn't have any friends as couples either, now we could.

I think this is a good time to answer the question you might be asking right now: "***if you resolved it, then you <u>resolved it</u>, get over it***" (2 Cor. 5:17 -

Therefore, if anyone is in Christ, he is a new creation; the old has passed away, the new has come!)

But remember from Chapter One I talked about being triggered? Or having something trigger me? What?!!!!!! I don't see that word in the Bible, as a matter of fact it sounded like the description of what Christians who didn't believe in Psychology based counseling called "Psychobabble"; that has proliferated in the Christian church over the last 30 years or so. There is the belief that all of life's situations are able to be solved with Bible verses and nothing more. (2 Pet 1:3 – His divine power *has given us everything we need for life and godliness* through our knowledge of Him who called us by his own glory and goodness). I was one of those who believed that concept by the *letter of the law*, not the *spirit* of it. Some of the Pastors of the churches we attended over the last 30 years believed the same way. There was little room for interpretation and application of the verses to help people solve their problems. As you will see in future chapters, God expanded that concept greatly in my life to be more in line with the spirit of the law not the letter of it. He had much more in store for my healing, (Isaiah 53:5 - But He was pierced for our transgressions, He was crushed for our iniquities; the punishment that bought us peace was upon him and by his wounds we are healed); for my victory over life's challenges (1 John 4:4 – You, dear children, are from God and have overcome them, because the One who is in you is greater than the one who is in the world); and the devil's attack on me and my family (Romans 16:20 – The God of peace will soon crush Satan under your feet).

Only 10 years ago, the type of reaction I had in that 12 step meeting to something totally unexpected, would have caused me such tremendous shame, fear, and humiliation that I would have had to run out of the place as fast as I could, and be afraid to ever go back. Fear of punishment and fear of rejection would not be far behind me as I ran. I would have physical panic attacks; those explosive fear causing, shaking, chest pains that made me feel like I was having a heart attack, sweating and feeling like I was going to die attacks. Wishing I would die so that the attacks would stop. I had been having several attacks a day for months in 1999 in all possible locations; like Sunday School, Church services, Wednesday night Bible Study, Saturday night prayer for revival, a sister in the Lord's house playing cards; any opportunity to cause disruption, and to cause people to think poorly of Christians or to expose Christians as phonies and hypocrites. I never wanted to bring shame to Jesus because of my behaviors. I don't believe Jesus ever had a panic attack! (Malachi 4:2-3 – But for you who revere my name, the sun of righteousness will rise with healing in its wings and you will go out and leap like calves released from the stall then you will trample down the wicked). There was a promise I could stand on!!!! I couldn't wait to see what God had in mind for my healing.

DISSOCIATIVE IDENTITY DISORDER

You may wonder just how I survived the events of my childhood. Of course, the answer is God. God gave my brain the ability to "store" the pain in another part of it in order to deal with the daily neglect and abuse that a 4 year old couldn't understand no less protect herself from. This ability is identified by the term Dissociative Identity Disorder. While this is a term many of you may have heard before, the name is most prominently used in reference to a Psychiatric diagnosis, I am referring to it as a spiritual condition. Each time that I faced a situation I didn't know how to handle I would unconsciously let another part of my brain to take over. That part would know what to do because it had been handling whatever situation I found myself in before for much of my life. This action is called shifting and is used by people with Dissociative Identity Disorder (DID). The process of creating an alter personality to which one could shift is called splitting.

I did not have a clue about this ability until I was 41 and had had so much counseling already that one of the counselors told me to get on with my life, and stop being a therapy "junkie". That fateful session with an Alcoholism Family Systems Therapist was when I was 33; for the next 10 years I sank my teeth into Christian practices such as faithfully attending church, reading, memorizing and meditating on the bible, as well as fasting, praying and fellowship which I was told were the missing links to living a victorious life. (Hebrews 4:12 – For the word of God is living and active, sharper than any double-edged sword. It penetrates even to dividing soul and spirit, joints and marrow; it judges the thoughts and attitudes of the heart). 2 Peter 1:3 - His divine power has given us everything we need for life and godliness through our knowledge of Him who called us by His own glory and goodness). And 2 Cor 3:18 – And we, who with unveiled faces all reflect the Lord's glory, are being transformed into His likeness with ever increasing glory which comes from the Lord, who is the Spirit.). I am not saying that all of this didn't change me. In fact it changed me a great deal. But even after being saved and discipled for many years by excellent teachers, I didn't have the abundant, victorious life that I read about in the bible. (John 10:10b – I have come that they may have life, and have it to the full).

So, even though I had done all I knew to do I found myself meeting with a Pastor and his wife "DR" & "CR", who specialized in prayer ministry; specifically inner healing and deliverance. What could inner healing do that all that counseling over the years and the practices of believers couldn't? What exactly was inner healing anyway?

Inner healing was another whole part of prayer ministry. In inner healing I opened my emotions to Jesus to bring healing so that the negative flashbacks, dreams and diversions that my brain took to escape the ever present pain would cease. When God first brought the idea of inner healing to my attention I was not interested. I was so very tired of telling the same sad stories of my childhood only to be told that I was cured when I wasn't. I was told to stop dwelling on the past, because I am a new creature now (2 Cor. 5:17 – Therefore, if anyone is in Christ, he is a new creation, the old has gone and the new has come). But inner healing is different I was told. I said: "I've survived this far without it, I don't need it". Nonetheless, I found my excuses melting under God's desires for my life and before I knew it I was at my first appointment.

You want to talk about God's desires? "DR" and "CR" his wife were only living here a few weeks and he didn't even have a space cleared yet to meet with people. That didn't stop us, however. We met anyway. I didn't know what to say to him, after all, he was a pastor and I was a "good Christian woman", (that was what I wanted him to believe anyway) and after all the antics of previous clergy I was really confused. All he had to do was ask me a few simple questions and explain the concept of "control" and as they say, "we were off to the races"! He told me to ask God for a couple of memories and after I completed the three questions he gave me to answer then he would see me again. Quick and simple. I was surprised at how fast and easy it went.

I was also surprised to find myself pondering the answer to such basic questions: Does God love me? Is God in control of the whole universe? Would he take care of me? I believed to a certain level that God loved me, same with would He take care of me. I was certain (though not understanding how) God controlled the whole universe.

And so it was time for my next appointment. During that appointment my belief that God loved me and was in control would be tested. I was asked to list basically all my "people": Father, mother, siblings, aunts and uncles, cousins, husband, children, etc. I was asked to list traumatic events from my childhood and all the sexual partners I had ever had (are ALL clergy so interested in SEX!!!???)

I wasn't able to finish listing everything during the allotted time so I took the questionnaire home and finished it there in preparation for the next appointment.

I was surprised at that appointment as I gave up control of everyone in my life now and ever in my life in the past; of the tears and emotion that sprang up and, of course, the pain. It was as though I had been trying to hold down many beach balls in a pool and couldn't keep them all down. One by one they started popping up in the pool. Lots of emotion I didn't know still existed came up.

"DR" and I didn't know it but various parts (short for parts of my brain, aka alters, assigned certain jobs for my functioning) of me were "coming up" and getting in touch with the pain and emotion that I pushed out of "me" into "them". They got a rotten deal out of my life. I will discuss this in detail later.

Once we were done the control ceremony it was time to begin the inner healing process with those memories that I had asked God to remind me of. But before that "DR" excused himself and then came back into the room and said that there was someone here who he knew and who wanted to come in the room and meet with me. He said it was Jesus.

I had what could be called a "meltdown". Instant hysteria, crying, lamentations, hiding my head under my arms, yelling NO, NO, NO, I am too dirty, too bad, too much of a disappointment. I didn't want Jesus to be embarrassed by me and my carrying on!!!! I had committed too many sins.

Little did I know that my reaction had just postponed the first healing time for me for several months. In the meantime I met with both "DR" and "CR" and serious talks about deliverance began. Part of that process was to read a book called "Deliver Us from Evil" by Don Basham. I began reading it and began to feel uncomfortable. By Chapter 11, the part where they tell you you HAVE demons, I was scared half to death. They said EVERYONE has demons because everyone grew up in this fallen world and what comes with the fallen world is sin. Our sin and the sins of our ancestors caused us to be cursed and traumatized by the people in the world with free choice. This gives entrance for demons to harass people, Christians included. If you recall from an earlier chapter I said there is a lot of disagreement and controversy about this, this is why.

I was on the phone to "DR" and found him not to be at home. That was ok because "CR" explained what had happened to me. The demons in me now knew that I knew they were in me and that their time to stay in me was short so they acted out. Fear is a demon; it produces the feeling of fear in humans. Yes, the flesh (soul) produces a feeling of fear and fear can be the result of a chemical imbalance and other reasons; and the demons WANT you to believe it is anything but them because they like it inside you, they get to experience humanity, feelings, and they stir up dissention inside people and to other people whose demons connect in the spiritual realm when people are together, to commit sin. Sin feels good many times but it kills the person slowly if not recognized for what it is (For the wages of sin is death. Romans 6:23).

So began the deliverance attempts. The first attempt was with all three pastors and their two wives present. They had me repent, renounce, forgive those who traumatized me and tell the demons in question that they HAD to leave. They vigorously informed the demons of their delegated authority from Jesus to bid them adieu and that they HAD to leave me. At the time I thought that perhaps there were no demons and this whole thing was a joke; shame was manifesting and I didn't realize it. I just started crying. They had me cough and cough and cough because they believed that demons are air beings, having no physical body; therefore they have to leave human beings via expulsion of air; usually from the mouth but also can be in the form of yawns, sneezes, belches, flatus (embarrasses the person involved; of course, demons hate them), very rarely vomiting or losing control of one's bladder (I did lose control of my bladder once and shame once again manifested). You have to *really* want them out of you. Not one went out of me that day. I was so humiliated I ran out of the room and didn't think I could ever face those people again. That reaction was from what was going on **inside of me** due to my past, not from what did or didn't happen that day. That experience triggered the problems from the past. This was not to be my last deliverance appointment, it was just the beginning.

Once the deliverance session was over, I had to pick up my middle daughter who was part of the youth group and had experienced deliverance herself recently. I was so ashamed to say that nothing happened. She was so good to me; she told me that not everyone gets the deliverance they want at every attempt. At 15 she had some wisdom already.

It was later discovered that the demons were able to stay because they had legal grounds (rights to stay); which were the wounds caused by the trauma of my early life. Until those wounds were healed the demons could stay. It was very frustrating to me. Even later on it was discovered that the demons were in my parts and that the requisite part wasn't up that day or at many of the other attempts at deliverance. When it was finally time for deliverance they had to leave and leave they did; but wound up bringing 7 demons worse than themselves back in with them.

How is this possible you want to know? With sufficient authority and by the power of the Holy Spirit (and fasting by me and/or the prayer team working on me) demons can be yanked out even though they still have grounds, but as I said they came back and brought 7 more demons with each one of them. I was one miserable woman afterward but I was suicidally depressed before that first appointment so I wanted to try to get healed and free despite the personal cost to me and my physical body.

What do I mean cost to my physical body? For at least two, if not three, days after a deliverance appointment I was wiped out. Wiped out meaning lying on the couch, sleeping as much as possible. My muscles all hurt from the effort expended trying to cough these fiends out of me. My stomach in particular would be sore as well from all the coughing. It took a toll on my mind; as I would walk around in a fog for several days. The Lord rescued me because I was working in an office part time during this period and many a day I couldn't concentrate because of the immense demonic pressure trying to make me kill myself or otherwise harm myself. Many, many a night I would not sleep long from the anxiety and still had to work the next day. My children were going crazy during this period of time acting out of rebellion. I had 3 under 20 which was worse than the 3 under 5 that I had when they were born!!!!

You might wonder why they were going crazy and exactly what going crazy means. Going crazy meant, for my oldest child, going to work full time for the first time, out of my purview as mother, in another town. Learning what "the world" is about from co-workers much older than her. Having sex for the first time, discovering internet pornography and phone sex. Getting willingly pregnant from a felon, winding up in jail for 18 days for shoplifting and more. We had to ask her to move out within two weeks of our notice to her of her unacceptable behavior. She was out in two days. Talk about distress. I didn't know where she was or with who. I had no phone contact for her.

While my oldest child was busy doing that, my younger two children also went crazy. The middle child went off to college but never was there. The college roommate reported her missing and the campus police called me to see if I knew where she was. I did know where she was because she had called me to tell me she was going out of state with a "friend" who was 14 years older than her who she met at her first "real" job, working in a pizza place. Her friend's husband owned the place. From there she disappeared because the "gig" was up. She was busted. She took the money we gave her for the second semester and spent it on drugs. She bounced from one "friend" to another, sleeping on couches. I had no idea where she was. I would hear that she was working in such and what restaurant and I would go there looking for her and of course, she wasn't on that night. Some places told me that if I made contact with her to tell her she was fired. I think she already knew that and that was why she didn't show back up. Finally she moved in with two or more men and several women. Everything in the apartment was sexually oriented. Things such as playing cards, lighters, phones, flashlights and things I thankfully can't remember She had become a raver (a person who attends Raves which are rock concerts where the drug Ecstacy (X) proliferates and creates a "love everyone" atmosphere) at that point with piercings, and tattoos. One day I went to visit her without calling her because I didn't have a phone number for her and she told me that if I ever did that again she would disappear and I would never hear from her again. She invited us to come to dinner (buy her dinner) for her 18th birthday and we went and took our pastor and his wife who she knew, and ate in one of those cook at your table Japanese restaurants. The food was good and it was good to see her and her friends. I couldn't believe she was my child. Shortly thereafter she moved to New Orleans. I wished her well.

And finally there was my third crazy child who at 17 began not coming home at night because he was staying with "friends" in another town who were also drinking and drugging in a tent or a condo. He was also engaged to one girl and having sex with another who became pregnant with our grandchild and eventually he married her. His insanity was short lived after having seen its toll on his older sisters!! There was still a period of time where I didn't know where he was. We had to tell him that if he was not going to be going to college that he needed to support himself and move out by the time he graduated high school as he would already be 18. He moved out on Father's Day of all days that year.

By the time the last child left home, the first one had given birth to a baby boy from the felon. It was so painful when she insisted on marrying him despite our pleadings not to do so. By the time that child was 3 months old; she was pregnant again, this time with a baby girl. She was legally married to him at this time. I thought it was a lot for her to handle but she was living with him and his parents so she had help. It was a mixed blessing because our oldest grandchild, a boy, drowned in that grandparent's swimming pool when or girl grandchild was 15 months old. Our girl grandchild gave my oldest child the need to continue to live despite her loss.

Evidently she still didn't understand that real life or should I say the life God had planned for her did not include Sex in the City type behavior. She graduated from a technical college and told me at the same time that she was pregnant again. This time she was pregnant without benefit of a man (not literally, just a sperm donor). She didn't want the trouble that comes from men cheating on her, beating her, getting her thrown into jail, using his pay for drugs while the children had no formula, etc. This child suffered asphyxiation as a result of a complete placental abruption at 34 weeks. He lived 31 hours. He was stillborn but they managed to resuscitate him for a brief period so that we could all say goodbye. He was baptized before he died by our pastor at the time.

The girl grandchild was approached by the brother of the woman her mother was sharing a home with and he tried to get her to let him see her pee pee. Thank God that was as far as it went. He went to jail and my daughter and her child moved 35 miles away from them to 5 miles from us. Praise God. After this event that daughter gave up trying to find a man. She entered therapy to find out why she HAD to have a man to survive and really learned a lot. God blessed her with the right husband and a little boy of their own after several years and at the time of the publishing of this book was pregnant again. She attends the church we now attend and even her husband came to church a few times. I am so happy for them. We take our granddaughter to church every Sunday morning.

Meantime, the middle daughter came out of the Raver lifestyle as she felt it might be time to grow up a little. Be responsible and have an apartment, go to school for real, and actually work a job not just say she had a job. A big improvement was made and we were so relieved. She was still using drugs big time however and I was always afraid that the phone would ring in the middle of the night and it would be the police saying that she had passed away. She wound up with a kidney infection that required her to get medicine she had no money for. We Western Unioned her the money for the doctor and drugs and then my husband set out on the road in his brand new pickup truck with my oldest child and her husband. They drove all night to New Orleans and packed her up and drove her back here right then. I was so glad. Then she met her current husband and began living with him. He was also had a drug and alcohol problem. Should we have known better? The good news was that he had been raised by very diligent parents with the same religious beliefs as us so we held out for a recommitment to Christ for him. Eventually she asked us to help her get clean and we did. A doctor in our church monitored her progress and treated her with whatever was necessary to get her clean. Her husband was not there yet at the time but at least he doesn't do heavy duty drugs anymore. She has finally gotten a good paying job working with children doing something she loves and her husband has a job he likes as well.

The third child moved in with us. He and his girl-friend and our girl grandchild. She was 7 months old by the time they moved in with us. I grew to love my daughter-in-law and my granddaughter. We bought a house big enough for both families and moved into that several years later. They go to church. We take our granddaughter to church with us most Sundays.

THE GOLDEN YEARS

When I was first saved I felt I had finally become something worthwhile and was a good wife and mother. At least I looked that way, and I actually believed it.

My children had God to save them, give them a hope, and security that I never had growing up. Salvation that is not earned and cannot be lost. But, unfortunately, because of my abuse as a child I became ultra-responsible and overprotective of them, (common in Adult Children of Alcoholics). You will see later the effects of my lack of security in my children.

By now you know I had a female child 3 years after the abortion, having spent those 3 years receiving counseling.

We looked for and found a house 45 miles from where we were living. My husband found a new job, day shift, and we moved from the big city to the suburbs. We were able to buy a tiny house, but it was a house and it would give a baby somewhere to live. There was no room in the apartment for a baby. The new house had a dog run and house in the yard, just what we needed because this dog needed exercise and a place to do dog things like dig.

Once we closed on the house I asked my husband if he was ready to have a child now and he said he was; so we began the practice of trying to get pregnant. It worked immediately and there was much excitement on his side of the family, my side – who cared? I, on the other hand was afraid of the unknown. I was morning sick all day long and throwing up several times a day so bad at one point that my boss couldn't take it anymore and sent me home. I was able to get medication from my doctor once I saw one and that stopped the vomiting but I was still round the clock nauseous and trying to survive each day until I was 3 months. It finally arrived and I had a good next three months, most women do. I was so conscious of my weight because of my father's preoccupation with women being fat. Forget it that he was fat, that was ok. In the seventh month of pregnancy I gained 5 pounds and was aghast; my doctor's partner yelled at me telling me to EAT, I had only gained 16 pounds so far in the pregnancy.

We had stopped going to church before the baby was conceived, as soon as I found out I was pregnant I started going back to church.

Within a year of buying that house we realized it was too small and so we put that one on the market and bought another one about 30 MORE minutes out into the country. We both had returned to college thanks to daycare. We had some classes together (very convenient) but as time went on there was less we could take together because we had different majors. But we did continue, with me during the day when daycare was available and with him at night after work. He graduated first and went on to a 4 year college to finish his degree in Business Administration, I had another baby and we moved and changed houses again and he changed jobs twice with nice raises in each move. God was providing for our exploding family, which would have continued except that I had a boy child. My husband told me I would be pregnant forever if I didn't have a boy, so I begged God for a boy. One morning I felt as though it might be the right day to conceive a boy and even though the last two children would only be 17 months apart I didn't want to start diapers all over again later so we took the plunge and 9 months later our son was born. His due date was one week earlier than when he arrived, but we knew when we had made him. So, I wound up with 3 children under five and one income. At least at that point we had joined a good church where God provided a spiritual mother for me and women's bible studies where all of us were in the same life circumstances. I learned a tremendous amount in those bible studies. Since I had not ever read the bible before, this was the time to do it and I did. Wow, there's all kind of stuff in there, good stuff. Some of the stuff completely contradicted what I was taught as a child, I found out I could KNOW that I was going to heaven, not just hope I was included in the "men" that Jesus died to save (John 6:47 - I tell you the truth that he who believes has everlasting life).

By the time my son was 2 and my daughters 3 1/2 and 6 I was starting to struggle again. These children were very active, already having very strong opinions of what they liked and didn't. There was a lot of fighting and spanking and I pushed myself well beyond what I ever thought was possible to be a good mother. And it wasn't until a couple of years ago that I realized that everything I claimed I had done was Jesus, it was grace. My life fell apart once my last child left home.

I was blessed with being able to enroll the oldest child in nursery school for several years and then she began full day kindergarten while my second-born began nursery school leaving me blissfully alone with just "the baby". By the time my oldest was in first grade she was on Ritalin for the same ADHD I suffered with undiagnosed those many years ago. Then the "baby" began nursery school and I was in frequent contact with the "sisters" that ran this particular daycare/nursery school. He was biting other children and told the sister that he didn't have to do what she said because she wasn't his mother. Believe me he got "what for" on the way home and my husband gave him a spanking and warned him to shape up. He had practice biting because my middle child bit him. They bit each other and the middle one bit me on the shoulder on the way out of church one Sunday and I thumped her on the mouth with a high intensity and a loud NO.

By the time my oldest was in second grade it became evident that she needed to go to school elsewhere. I had wanted to put her in Christian School from day one, indeed the middle child's nursery school was the one run by our church and she went on to Christian School for first grade. Her birthday fell one day after the public school cut off for the year and there was NO WAY she was going to do ANOTHER year of nursery school. The teachers at the nursery school and the daycare at the college where I was going all agreed she needed to move on. Since the public school wouldn't take her we checked into the Christian school. They made their own rules and they took her. I loved it there for her, she flourished.

In second grade my oldest child got the "teacher from hell". She treated the second graders like college students, expecting way too much from them. After several meetings with the teacher and the principal we decided to put her in Christian school with her sister. She stayed on the Ritalin and did well. My third born joined his sisters in Kindergarten and the teacher/principal told me he was hyperactive and needed Ritalin. I was not happy about it, one of my children was already on Ritalin and now I was going to add my 5 year old as well? I struggled a lot with that situation; indeed, I wound up in a depression I didn't know I had but affected my ability to deal with the stress I was under. It doesn't sound like what I described would be considered very stressful but I left out the DSS part.

EXPERIENCES WITH DSS

Yes, we were reported to the state agency that makes sure children are not neglected or abused not once, *but twice*. Let's go backward for a minute, shall we? My first born wound up on Ritalin but not before we went through the mandatory "home study" and psychological and learning disability testing. A Social Worker from the county came to our home (hence, the term home study) and asked all kinds of questions. She was with us for hours. I felt invaded and worried about what she would report. When the learning testing was done it was revealed that my oldest child had a high I. Q. (most ADHD kids do) but that she was "perceptually impaired". What the heck that meant I didn't have a clue but it did entitle her to individualized teaching in the "Resource Room". I was thrilled to have individual work for her but I should have listened to my husband's older brother about the stigma that would attach to her that she was "one of THOSE kids, the stupid, retarded ones". Also because of her designation she had "group" therapy with the school psychologist weekly. I spoke to the psychologist several times as well because I was still at war with my husband. I wanted him to get help and he wouldn't. I couldn't make him.

And then, one day I was at a muffler shop getting the muffler replaced on my car when the 3 kids were going bonkers, fighting with each other, screaming, falling down on the floor, chasing each other, pretty "everyday" behavior for them. I was desperately trying to get control of them before we got thrown out of the place. I was forbidden to bring my children with me when I went to get my allergy shots weekly because when I was there they tore up the waiting room in a similar manner. I was only going there a few weeks when I got a letter telling me the above. I was afraid this was going to happen again so I pulled the oldest one aside and told her that if she didn't cut it out and behave I was going to put her in the bathroom when we got home. The pediatrician had just recently told me to put her in there when she refuses to obey and that it might takes days before she begins behaving. So, when I got her home I put her in the bathroom as I promised if she didn't behave and she didn't. I had to remove everything I could out of the room because she was destroying the room while she was in there. Hour after hour, day after day and then the doorbell rang. I answered it and there was this man, in his 20's I thought with a briefcase. He told me who he was and what he was and asked me if I had ever heard of DSS. I told him that I knew they gave gifts to poor children every Christmas but that was about all. I made the mistake of letting him in without my husband or an attorney there which I remedied quickly with phone calls. He began to ask me questions about our family and how we disciplined the children and I told him exactly what the pediatrician had told me. He asked to see the closet where my oldest had been kept. I told him it wasn't a closet, it was a bathroom and that the door didn't lock, it had no lock on the doorknob to lock. I even called the pediatrician's office 911 and begged them to put him on the phone to set this DSS guy straight. They were on the phone for a few minutes and then he gave me the phone back and the doctor told me that I had misunderstood him. He meant that the children could be put in "time out" for 5 minutes or more each time they violate a rule but must be let out each time the time is up. When he said it might take days he meant the repetition may take several days to convince them to behave. In NO WAY did he mean to put any child in that stripped down bathroom for DAYS with no toys or diversion. I brought her food to her each meal and she slept in her bed but that was it. I thanked him for his time and hung up. I was so embarrassed, but more than that I was terrified they would take my children away from me. I was already struggling with their outlasting me and being stronger; it was the three of them against just me and this was going to make it worse. It was agreed that I could keep the children but that I had to have a psychological evaluation by the state, by both a psychologist and a psychiatrist. My husband and daughter had to be evaluated also. There was no way on this earth I was going to allow them to talk to my child alone. There was no way for me to be able to be sure that they would not manipulate her (she was only 4 or 5) or scare her (she didn't know them from a hole in the wall). I asked if I was allowed to use my own psychologist and psychiatrist; they were fine with that but when I inquired of a Christian psychologist and psychiatrist it was going to cost us $1,200 for them to do what the state was demanding. I just started to cry and couldn't stop. I was terrified. Having been abused as a child there was no way that I would abuse them and yet I was held accountable for their behavior. Somehow I was supposed to magically convince them to do as I asked (and society asked). Once the man from DSS left, I called the only attorney I knew, the one that did the closing on my home. My attorney at that point referred me to another attorney in their firm. This one dealt with family law only. He told us to cooperate fully because if we didn't they would have a court order to remove our children instantly. I was absolutely furious. Someone in that muffler waiting room told a lie and it led to an investigation and all kinds of government interference into how I raise my kids. So, eventually the day came when we all had to see the state appointed mental health professionals. I was astounded, the psychologist told me he was on my side and that I didn't have to be afraid. He had worked for the state but he wanted to help the parents that get pulled into this government circus wrongfully. I naively believed him and told him what he wanted to know. He told me that it sounded like my child was hyperactive and asked if I had ever considered that or been told that by anyone and I hadn't. He explained that was why she didn't obey; her nervous system was short circuited so she flitted from one thing to another without even thinking what the consequences might be. All my talking just went over her head. He also had me take a depression test and I answered so many of them positively he said I was clinically depressed. That was why it was so hard to deal with the three of them. I found out later that the last child was also hyperactive, but he was 5 by the time I found that out. Next came the meeting with the psychiatrist. I don't know if he spoke with the psychologist or not but he gave me a prescription for an anti-depressant and told me to follow up with my family doctor. He did NOT seem to be on my side like the psychologist, I was glad to get out of there. I was allowed to watch thru a one way mirror as the doctors questioned my child. I could not hear but at least I could see that they did not touch her or in anyway violate her as I was violated as a child. The DSS worker had told us that he would be back to check on us monthly or something and then we never saw him again. That was God's mercy towards us.

We saw God's mercy again the second time DSS showed up at our door. This time I didn't let her in but called my attorney and told the DSS lady she would have to wait until he got there before I spoke to her. I also called my husband who came home from work. At that point in time I had been prescribed Zanax for anxiety along with my antidepressant and was encouraged to take it by my doctor. This time around I had no idea why the state agency was there. I hadn't done anything inappropriate. I didn't have to convince the state agency worker of that, the complaint was against my husband for supposedly physically molesting my oldest child. It turned out the school psychologist whom I had talked to about how I was struggling in my marriage and with my husband who wouldn't get help reported him. She showed my child an anatomically correct doll and told the psychologist that her daddy tickled her "there". She asked her to point to where her daddy did that and the psychologist says that my child indicated her private parts. I told that state agency worker that that school psychologist was nuts. I was ALWAYS there when they had what we called "the tickle wars". He tickled all three kids, they loved it and jumped on and tried to tickle daddy back. I told the worker to go ask the children. My attorney went with her into another room where they were questioned and seemed satisfied with the information she received. I believe the school psychologist was trying to be helpful and thought she saw a way to force my husband to get help (or lose his kids). The reason I told her about our marriage was because the Pastor of our new church had met with us a few times and told me that I wasn't a submissive wife and that I needed to submit and then there wouldn't be all the fighting and problems. The more I submitted the more he demanded and controlled me. I just kept thinking if I could be a good enough wife he would treat me better. He didn't and I felt that because of the children I had to keep trying.

I had switched attorneys since the first state agency call because I was not at all happy with the previous attorney's help. By this point we were in a new church and there was an attorney in the choir in which we sang and we asked him to be our attorney. He did a good job and we were very grateful. We never heard from the state agency again. I was so upset that I popped one of my Zanax without realizing it was double the strength I was used to taking and so I was knocked out for the next 12 hours, my husband had to figure out what to do with the children for dinner and bedtime and breakfast and off to school and still go to work the next day. He might have thought I was dead but if he shook me hard enough I would mumble something at him and go back to sleep.

Because of the above incidents I was given the opportunity along with my husband to have "prayer counseling". This was a method developed by one of the mainline denominations that helped Christians with their difficulties through prayer. This was not inner healing; as a matter of fact they didn't believe in Inner Healing, they thought it was really a New Age method. Obviously I went along with them at that point and had the prayer counseling. What it amounted to was tons of legal work to take away the rights (grounds) of any demons that were in me due to this DSS trauma so that they would have to leave when told and I told them to leave. There was no visible manifestation to denote their leaving but I did feel better.

After this event, we moved the oldest child to the Christian School, so all three of my kids went there. I was so glad. We didn't have the money for the tuition but God provided me a part time job that I loved which paid the tuition but I had to work through the summer. I put the children in that Daycare run by the Roman Catholic sisters but there is quite a difference when you are the adult not the child; but I kept an eye on them anyway interrogating the oldest child each day about what they had done all day. By the end of the summer the youngest one had gotten the concept of no biting and even if they are not your parents you must obey authority over you.

Don't get the idea that the youngest child became an angel at that point because he didn't. I was at home early one fall morning when I got a phone call from the Catholic grade school on their bus route that my oldest child was there bleeding out of her head. They needed me to come get her. I went and was praying the whole time over there. Turns out my "angel" had hit his oldest sister with his metal lunch box on the back of her head which left a nasty gash and as we all know, head wounds bleed like crazy. He was gone with his other sister on the bus and it was a good thing because he would have gotten pounded but good for that stunt. She needed stitches, but at that point I was an expert at stitches because this same child had jumped off a piece of 5 foot high furniture and cracked her head on the way down to the floor at my next door neighbor's house. Even with a towel you could follow the blood trail from my car through the ER to the bed where she was sitting with ice now over the washcloth that they put on there until she got stitched up. When my middle child was about 3 she ran into the end of our new wood sofa and split the front of her face open above the eyebrow and had to be stitched up. You could see her skull, it was that deep. Turns out God put a nurse with her that was very kind and the doctor stitched her up without a lot of screaming. You can barely see the scar. She wound up with a bandage that we nicknamed The Red Badge of Courage because the nurse put a big red cross over the top of the bandage on the front of her head.

Just because we are already talking about that day I will tell you about what the youngest child did about 5 minutes after the middle one did that. He stuck a metal hanger into his eye. YEP, right in front of me stuck the hanger into his eye. I was ironing and had just made some kind of comment to my husband about kids sticking hangers into their eyes. I screamed and ripped the thing out of there (not too bright a move on my part). And, if that wasn't enough, we adults both had the flu and were down ourselves. Of course it doesn't matter if you are dead, you still have to take the children to the hospital to get stitches and get their eyes checked out and we did, his eye was fine, no scratching of the lens took place.

One day I was on my way to my part time job while the children were in school and within seeing distance to my destination I was hit head on by a panel truck. I had been praying when it happened and didn't know what had happened. There were a lot of people around there and some of them came up to me to ask who they could call and to tell me not to move until the EMS got there. Turns out that the truck that hit me was coming down a hilly curve and didn't see the lane in front of him was stopped.

So, he swerved into what he thought was an open passing lane, the lane I was in and hit me. Neither of us was going very fast but there was enough damage that it totaled the car. We filed a claim against his insurance and received a small settlement because I only had soft tissue damage, but it came at a very good time and helped us buy a replacement car. I was out of work only a few days and went back to work as I had before the accident.

Only 17 months later I was driving to my sister's bridal shower and I noticed that there was a car going very slowly in the 4th and outermost lane of the bridge I was driving over. I realized he was an accident waiting to happen so I moved over one lane to the right and was hit by a car going 90 mph or more for all I know. What I do know is that I was hit so hard that it accelerated me into the car in front of me. I had both feet on the brakes and still hit the car. I managed to get my car over the bridge to the right shoulder out of danger and got out of the car to see how the people were in the other car. The woman was madder than a mad hatter because I said to her that I recognized her customized license plate as they passed me on the inside. She thought I hit them because I was looking at their license plate instead of at the road when I told them I had been rammed and that is what forced me into them. Someone had called the police and as I waited I showed them the back of my minivan with the bumper pushed in and the floor pushed up. I was looking for my eyeglasses; I was hit so hard that they flew off my face onto the floor in the corner of the passenger side. I couldn't see much of anything without them. The police arrived and God blessed me because the officer was the "little" brother of a girl that was in my class when we graduated from high school. I asked him if he was related to her and he told me he was her brother and that she had twins. Of course the people who I hit were not very happy with this cop talking to me about his sister. They wanted their pound of flesh. He did not ticket me and asked me if I needed medical assistance. I thanked him and told him I didn't have any bad injuries so I continued on (the car was drivable) to the shower and was late. I told the ladies what happened and they offered me ice and ibuprofen and I took it.

The next morning I woke up very sore and bruised, my neck hurt from the whiplash from the accident. I proceeded to get adjustments by my chiropractor and physical therapy for months but I didn't get better. They tried to hold my job for me because I was a very good worker but eventually, after 6 months, I resigned so that they could fill my position. They needed someone to service my accounts.

I was taking business courses in college at this point and during one of them, Business Law, there was a section about filing a claim with your own insurance for pain and suffering from a hit and run. That is what it is for. I proceeded to call my attorney the next day and he confirmed I could do so and he filed it for me. I did receive a small settlement because all I had was soft tissue damage and God had the settlement arrive exactly when we needed it, because my husband was laid off from his job and was out of work for 8 months while we had 3 young children and I was homeschooling them. I made the choice to stay home with them rather than work to have more money. After I had made that choice I decided to home school. It turned out to be the right choice because I lost the job that paid their tuition and my husband wasn't working either.

The reason I decided to home school was that my oldest child had adjusted to Christian School until the 6th grade at which time she became the student that didn't fit. All her classmates were doctors and lawyers kids, dual income families with the latest fashions and big fancy everything. We chose NOT to live that way; we relied on God for their clothes, our house, etc. And, God did supply in a number of ways. Once in a while the children would have the latest fashions from connections I had with mothers whose girls were a little bit older and sold me their girls' things; garage sales and their grandparents for their birthdays. Just not everything they ever wanted. We were trying to raise them with the values of Jesus. With the classroom situation the way it was, my oldest child's best friend started being home schooled. Her parents were not very happy with the classroom situation either. Without her best friend in the class, my oldest was all alone and it became very painful for her. I visited her best friend and her mother as we had known them a few years and while we were there I observed how they were home schooling. It wasn't that far out, nothing I couldn't handle, so my oldest became home schooled that September. I brought the other two children home to school in November during Thanksgiving break. It was a good thing I did because there was no way to pay their tuition. I felt it was a blessing. God had given us so many blessings.

Little did I know as I blissfully homeschooled those children that first year that we would soon be moving to the deeeeep south. Actually, homeschooling became a source of security for our children. It was portable, could be moved anywhere without any loss of continuity. They still had the same teacher, me, and the same classmates, their siblings. They could skip all that angst which usually accompanies moving not just in state where at least some things are familiar but to another state 1200 miles away from anything familiar (including grandparents and other relatives). To be honest there wasn't much of a relationship with any of our relatives because we were Christians and most of them weren't. Also, my father was of the school of "I raised mine, now you raise yours" (truth was he didn't raise us, he abused us and I was glad to move away because he undermined what we were trying to teach our children). His moral compass was turned the complete opposite way. An example of that with my children was his insistence on watching R rated movies when we visited him once a month, his swearing in their presence, his statements that I should have aborted at least one of them. But, he was their grandfather and I had to honor him by visiting. Truth was that I was trying to gain the acceptance I never got in childhood (my issue, not his).

I know I made it sound easy for us to move to the Deep South, but it was anything but that. My husband had taken a 15% pay cut at his job one year before we moved. Everyone did because the company had a no lay off policy. The following year he was laid off along with a Vice President and 5 other highly paid employees. So much for the no lay off policy. The Lord did take care of us with 6 months of severance pay, three weeks of vacation and 6 months of health care after which we could COBRA it to keep it in effect. During those 6 months was the hardest time in the real estate market where we lived in the last 25 years. We were told we would have to take a loss because of all the other houses on the market that were just as nice as ours. It did not happen that way only because the Lord intervened. We had a Christian couple come and make us an offer and before the ink was dry we received another offer from a different couple who had CASH to pay for the house. Our realtor (a church member) advised us to take the cash offer. We didn't want to but if the other people didn't get a mortgage then we would be out in the cold again. We were all ready to sign the final contract when we saw there was an addendum requiring us to make $25,000 of repairs to the house. The house was only 10 years old and we took excellent care of it. There was no way that it could need that much repair. Besides, our listing said it was for sale "AS IS" which meant that we were not going to spend 1 cent on repairs. So, our realtor relayed our answer.

The next day we received the offer back with stipulations for $20,000 of repairs. This went on for two weeks with us each time saying that the house was for sale "AS IS". Finally we asked our lawyer if we had to continue to fight with these people because we needed to sell the house NOW as we were moving. The lawyer relayed the message to their lawyer that as of 2 pm that Friday the house would be released back onto the market. The next morning (Saturday) at 9 am the house was sold again this time to the nice Christian couple. Yes, they had to get a mortgage but we were ok with that.

Come Monday morning my husband gets a phone call from the other buyers and they couldn't understand what had happened, he thought we had a contract. My husband asked him what part of "AS IS" he didn't understand and terminated the call. As an aside, this person also bid on another house in our neighborhood at the same time as ours and they sold theirs to someone else evidently because he was trying the same tactics on them. He got what he deserved.

We knew we were moving but did not know where. My husband had a job interview in Wisconsin so we thought we were moving there. We had a realtor sending us listings from there. Then we were looking at houses in the state we were in because he had a job offer 2 hours south of where we currently lived. We received a phone call from a recruiter the week before asking us if he was still looking for a job and he asked them what they had and it was a job in the Deep South. So, most of our possessions had been packed and in the garage for two months as the silliness with the sale of the house and the indeterminate location of his new job continued. Finally, the day before we were going to sign a lease to rent a house we couldn't afford in the state we lived in to be closer to that job 2 hours south of us, he was offered the job in the Deep South. This was now Christmas and he had to report January 2nd. The moving company came the day after Christmas and packed the Christmas tree still decorated and put it into the moving truck. What a rush, how fearful. God had told us at the beginning that we were going to be like Abraham, and move, but had not told us where we were going. It felt like a wilderness to us.

Anyway, we showed up to our rental condo and were amazed by the total culture change we experienced. 85 degrees in January, people in shorts, children never having to go inside their houses at night because it was so warm. Yes, it was dark, but there were streetlights at the corners and the darkness provided the perfect atmosphere to play what they called "Manhunt". It basically was hide and seek in the dark. This ability to play outside year round gave me no respite from their activities and I wound up exhausted. At our previous location there were very defined seasons. It became too cold and raw, wet and uncomfortable to be outside once the sun went down and it went down early where we lived. 4:30 pm in December. So, all activity slowed down and became watching TV, playing video games and doing homework. It gave me a break from having to run them all over creation for all their activities. In this new place their activities were more in the winter because it was so hot in the summer. Plus, in the old location, we didn't have the availability of 24 hour a day activities. In this place we did. The bowling alleys and movie theatres never closed, neither did several of the restaurants and retail stores so there was ALWAYS something to do at any hour of the day or night. The home school group we joined was huge and there were plenty of educational activities for the children to participate in as well as the town's recreation program which I was talking about above. Eventually I became responsible for the "teen" portion of the activities of the home school group and I planned all the activities for them for the entire year. We wound up going behind the scenes at Sea World, to NASA at Cape Kennedy so they could see behind the scenes of the space program and to the Miami Seaquarium as well. It was one of the high points of my life.

While we were there we found ourselves self employed. A woman in one of the churches that we attended had a cleaning business she had to give up and we took it over. We had a great time. All three children had their part of the cleaning job and because of that we could clean more houses per day and make more money. I used the job as part of our schooling by incorporating into it mathematics, economics, home education, etc. We still did the regular school work for as long as needed each day. While we were living there we made liberal use of our close prox-imity to several amusement parks. They had resident day rates and since we were residents we took advan-tage of them.

This was so different from the country atmo-sphere we had been in for the previous 20 years. At first we knew no one in our new location. My husband had a new job for a company that was one of the primary providers of employment in that state and it turned out that his boss was similar to Simon Legree. My husband was miserable every work day. Since they had moved us they insisted on his signing a one year contract which stated that if he quit before one year was over we would have to pay back all that they spent to move us. He figured he could do ANYTHING for a year so he signed it. Boy was he blindsided. This boss threatened him with his job every day for a year just because he could. My husband was doing an adequate job but this boss was power hungry and knew how to tap into people's insecurities. Eventually he got a new boss and his old boss was reassigned because no one would work for him (I wonder why).

Since we lived such a short distance from the ocean we took advantage of it during the day when only the tourists were there. This was a mixed blessing. I had never seen such clear beautiful aqua colored water and such white sand in my life. The water was as warm as my bath water and we could see the fish swimming around beneath us and sometimes they nibbled our feet. We even were blessed enough to have the children have an encounter with baby dolphins as they snorkeled with their father in the ocean. Just about every house had its own pool and the owners were kind enough to let our children swim in them.

After the third time or so of scorching sunburn regardless of how much sunscreen we used we began to put t shirts over them when going in the ocean.

Something about the salt water must have been deci-mating that suntan lotion rendering it ineffective. Pools became their place to swim. We would still go to the ocean later in the day or early in the morning because the sun was either lower in the sky on the ocean or the other side so we could walk and even swim for a little while.

One of my functions as the home school teen program leader was finding places that were educa-tional as well as just fun. My personal favorite was the library. The libraries there were unbelievably big and had recently published books. In our old library the books were quite old with very few recently published up to date ones. I never wanted to leave these libraries (there were several like the one I am describing each a little further away from our house, but wonderful just the same). We biked most every-where which included to these libraries because we now lived in a city where everything was blocks and blocks intersected by traffic lights and stop signs a plenty. Cars were a plenty also. But along with the throngs of people were throngs of shopping opportu-nities. Just the supermarkets were astounding. There was one at almost every corner!!! The newspaper said that each resident had .6 mile of mall space to their very selves!!! Amazing. So much variety, so much choice, such great deals. We went to the brick and mortar stores and also to the outside "flea markets" where the deals were the best. There was even a children's ride section outside and a circus ride or two on the inside in the food court with a live perfor-mance every other hour. Amazing. Golf and fishing were also amazing. That was how I talked my father into coming to visit. He and my husband played golf and went fishing all winter long. Of course, it rained every day at 2 pm or so but that never stopped them. He also enjoyed the authentic south pacific restaurant in the town near us where a show was included with dinner (expensive but worth it) and a little "show club" just up the street from us provided entertainment while we ate as well. It had a 40's cabaret act and there was dancing there after the show. I loved it as I loved to dance.

The children had their own love called the "Grand Prix". It was a huge indoor arcade with every game and pinball or participatory activity you could ever image. A lot like the huge one of its kind at Disney World, it had its own laser tag and go carts, etc. And Grand Prix wasn't the only place like this. There were others one nicer than the first one all over our area within miles of each other. We loved it.

INDECENCY

It was hard to get used to so many people living so close to one another, the lines at almost everywhere, having to show my license every time I used a credit card and the public nudity. There was a woman or should I say women who had hot dog carts next to a main highway under a bridge. They towed their hot dog carts with their Mercedes. Hot dogs were $5 each without soda or toppings or chips but that didn't matter because people were paying for the VIEW not the food. The police reported that the accident rate at that location tripled the accident rate anywhere else in that area because the truck drivers lost control of their rigs and crashed into the side of the road or each other. You guessed it; the hot dog vendors looked naked. They weren't but they looked like they were. It looked like they used dental floss as a bathing suit and believe it or not there were no statutes that they were violating. They were a tourist attraction and brought money into the economy. This area had to compete with the Riviera in France where toplessness and full nudity are tolerated.

Speaking of toplessness, we were "privileged" to experience that at a certain famous beach on Memorial Day one year. I had always wanted to see that famous beach and so on a hot and sunny day we went there. We weren't familiar with exactly every detail of the area so we parked and started walking toward the sand. I could see that some women were lying on their stomachs with their bathing suit top undone but I had seen that at beaches everywhere so I didn't think much of it until they turned over and left the suit off. I almost passed out. I had the three kids (10, 11, and 13) with me and I couldn't move fast enough to shield them. We kept moving and tried to find a place where there wasn't nudity. I finally thought I found it so we put down our blanket and were looking at the beautiful aqua water and the cruise ships docked across the way from where we were. Next thing I knew this young woman was coming up out of the water in a tee shirt. I thought to myself how sleazy, she ought to know better. She did know better all right, just not what I thought she should know. She grabbed hold of the bottom of the wet see- through shirt and pulled it off. She resembled Mae West and I started screaming to my husband that we were leaving. He hadn't seen what I saw and so he was startled but started to move anyway. I had my girls block my son's vision on both sides and had him look down as we led him to the car. My girls could see what was going on and they called it gross, which it indeed was. So much for my enjoying that place!!! We never went back there again, and I was embarrassed that I exposed my children to that indecency. We did try again to go swimming. This time we drove all the way down the coastline to a state park where there were guided snorkeling excursions. The people there had their clothes, but the women on the beach were topless. I asked the ranger about it and he said there *were* statutes on the books against this, as a matter of fact, they have a designated and well marked nude beach but people use the entire beach topless. The problem was that there was no enforcement and if there was no enforcement nothing changes. They finally temporarily "solved" the hot dog lady situation by requiring them to provide rest rooms because they are restaurants. They disappeared for a short time but reappeared a little further down the road with portable bathrooms pulled behind their hot dog carts!!!!

We found the people who lived in this location "on vacation" all the time. They didn't cook, they didn't know their neighbors and didn't want to know them. They evidently were running from people, the law or themselves. Needless to say that left us kind of lonely. Even the church people were different, kind of sophisticated, dressed to the nine's and made up to perform in the theatre. I was out of place without make up in Wal-Mart clothes. My kids' clothes were hand me downs or thrift shop clothes (what else do you need for homeschooling)?

Speaking of churches, it is quite a story how we wound up attending our first church there. On a Sunday we had gone to a church that we had never gone to before of the Assembly of God denomination. It was a small church but seemed to have the familiar markers of our beliefs. We left praying about whether we should go back or not.

The next day there was a knock at the door at 7:00 pm and a very nice looking, very nicely dressed and very charismatic gray haired man introduced himself as Pastor ABC of DEF church. He asked if he could come in and chat a moment with us and we invited him in. He asked us how we liked the service, the sermon; the friendliness of the people, if we were saved (snuck that one in there). He went on and on about what the church had to offer: a 100 member High School youth group, a similarly numbered jr. high youth group, a children's group, a 100 member choir; in other words, the church of my dreams. We had always been in small churches and never had a big youth group or choir. There were numerous adult Sunday school classes there which had many subjects to study and numerous activities to take part in. I found it odd that I didn't see all this at church that morning and so I asked the pastor where this church was located and he said at such and such and such and such streets. It was then that I asked what the name of the people that he was here to visit was. Needless to say, it wasn't us but the family that had occupied our temporary lodging before us. It didn't matter though, God had spoken and we had found a new home for our church family. They even had huge production events that were broadcast on the local cable system whose president was a member of that church. The Easter play brought me to tears. I actually felt like I shook Jesus' hand, not the actor's. We didn't have speaking roles, we were the choir.

Even the children were in it. It was a once in a life-time experience for which we still thank God today.

It was a good thing that we loved that church because that was where we were attending when my sister's AIDS became final stage and she eventually died from the complications of it. She was so young with a young child and husband that she left behind. It was too bad that she got involved with the wrong type of man and had turned away from God years earlier. I thanked God that she did not get all the manifestations of the disease, many of which were unsightly and painful; although she did get enough to be in much pain and drop to 76 pounds before she died. She looked like she was 90 not 34. She had had two children, one of which progressed to full blown AIDS at age 2 and a second child who was also full blown AIDS at 5 months and passed on at that time from complications of AIDS. As a Christian it caused me tremendous doubt in my God and my faith. I really believed that God would heal her (by His stripes we are healed) and when He chose to heal her by taking her home and giving her a whole new body I was crushed and angry. If God did not hold me close until I could see straight again I would have walked away from Him. How little I understood about God. I can see that now that I am growing older and have drawn closer to God in my relationship with Him.

As I explained above, we wound up in a church we never visited because we felt God wanted us there and He did. 9 months later we missed the Spirit filled part of our faith and so we moved to an Assembly of God church in the same town. Talk about spirit filled.

This pastor really believed in the use of the gifts of the spirit and was very spirited in his preaching. Unfortunately, he was a little too enthusiastic and we wound up leaving there after 9 months to an Independent Baptist Church. Someone said we went there to HIDE, and that if The Holy Spirit were to move there everyone would know it!!!!!

Still, it was a place of rest and predictability. We enjoyed the pastor's preaching and got saved 4,336 times in the 18 months we were there. (Can you take a joke?) The people there were real. Have you over to their house for dinner real; go to the movies or to mini golf with the kids real, able to talk to them real. We finally found what we wanted and the best part was it was recommended by someone in our home school group that I still keep in contact with today. They fit in with what we were teaching our children in school. And then it was time to move north again. The job with Simon Legree was over and we were free to leave.

But it took a little more effort to move out of there than to have relocated there. We started taking the Sunday Edition of out of state newspapers in January, and in September there was an ad in the paper for our town that was as if it had copied my husbands resume exactly. He immediately applied and heard NOTHING. For months, NOTHING. We figured at that point that they had hired someone else when the phone rang and it was them. They wanted him to come for an interview over Thanksgiving and so he did. He felt that he would be a good fit and that they liked him as well. We looked forward to getting out of the Deep South soon. Thank you God for answered prayer.

Except that Christmas went by and then Valentine's Day and still nothing. In the meantime my husband had minor surgery with a major side effect which put him back in the hospital 10 days. He was on crutches when he went for that interview but he left them in the hotel room. All he needed was to be seen as disabled, forget that job. March 1st came and they finally called and offered him the job which he accepted. We had 30 days to sell our house and move as he started April 1st. Forget about that he would be back to work for only two weeks before he would give them notice of his leaving. In some ways it was too bad that we were moving, my husband's new boss was super good. In fact, he put our airplane tickets to go to my sister's funeral on his credit card since all our sources of money but cash were frozen until the new cards/bank account was ready. Two weeks after the funeral I got a phone call from hospital security telling me that they found my purse in the cleaning closet around the corner from my late sister's room. I knew that cleaning woman had taken it, I just couldn't prove it. The only thing that she took was the cash (ha ha on her, I carry very little to no cash on me).

Overall, moving was the right thing to do. We had the police being called for our neighbors down the block because she was drunk and he was beating her. Their son sold drugs. The boy two houses down who was younger than my youngest child was watching "Real Sex" on HBO (I only found this out after we moved). A teacher was stabbed at the local high school and they put in metal detectors as early as 1993. There was gang activity around the corner from us and a shooting one day. I was *very happy* to home school and have the children involved in swim team, soccer, basketball, gymnastics, horseback riding, bowling and home school activities as well as church functions. They were accompanied by me everywhere they went. We were able to participate in many activities there that we would not have been able to participate in any other home school group except maybe in California.

We put the house up for sale and within the 30 days we had a buyer but he couldn't get a mortgage. Thankfully, the new company paid our mortgage for 6 months as it wound up taking a year before we could close. The realtor arranged for the buyer to rent from us after 6 months to pay the mortgage since they had moved in right after the first 30 days.

When we moved we told the phone company to discontinue our phone on that Monday as they wouldn't do it on Saturday and we needed it until then. We left on Sunday morning and when we received our phone bill there was $1,000 worth of calls to the islands which we didn't make. Some one took a phone and jacked it into our exterior box and made those calls. We had to do quite a bit of convincing and proving that we didn't make those calls. The phone company did eventually remove the charges, thank you Jesus.

NIRVANA

This move we decided not to buy a house immediately. We signed a lease for a year in a beautiful two story colonial with a fully wooded yard in a very exclusive executive development. We were on the cul de sac. Not a lot of traffic coming through this street or noise from the neighbors either. Don't get me wrong, the people (when we saw them) were friendly enough, that is just the southern way. It took a while to learn what the southern way was. The vocabulary alone took years to learn and getting used to being asked every time I opened my mouth "you're not from around here are you?" No, I'm from up north, but I got here as fast as I could!!!! (I didn't dare say that last part as southerners think that Yankees are loud, aggressive, and intellectually superior to them).

What a wonderful place to have moved. I would sit outside on the front stoop and just listen to the quiet. Or the peepers, (frogs that sound like birds) that start peeping in the late winter (January here in the DS), spring is in February or March here. There were also the cicadas. They are everywhere and are very noisy when the weather is hot and muggy. I also experienced my first tulip popular tree where the leaves look like tulips and my first honeysuckle vine (intoxicatingly beautiful).

The particular year we moved I swore I moved from the Deep South to the north. The weather was uncharacteristically cold, it snowed 3 times that winter (a record I think) and the snow stayed on the ground. They closed the schools for the rest of winter (only kidding) but they did close them a lot because people there did not know how to drive in anything other than sun and maybe rain.

Remember the beautiful two story colonial we rented? It evidently had no insulation. It certainly felt like it. There was electric baseboard heat which is the most expensive form of heat and when we received the first bill we almost fainted, and so it became our goal to reduce that bill. I put on every piece of clothing I owned and still froze. I thought my blood had thinned out living where we had previously so I also had to overcome that as well. We had a kerosene heater that we had purchased when we were up north that I dragged in from the garage and used. There was a fireplace that did not have a heatilator so it wasn't much good, but we used it anyway. We closed off the vents for the air conditioning in the other rooms to keep the cold from sinking in and the heat from escaping. We put towels against the bottom of the doors to stop the cold from coming in. We basically lived in the kitchen which had doors on both sides or left one door open wishfully thinking that the fire-place would help us out in the kitchen.

Actually, our two dogs proved to be quite helpful at 50 pounds each, we had them sit on us to keep us warm. They put out quite a bit of heat!!!! The low one morning was 16 degrees with a wind chill of below zero. I swore I was in the north because of the cold and the snow. Oh, and I forgot to mention, the ice. We didn't characteristically get much snow there every winter, but we did get ice storms. Power would go out. We have gas logs in our current house so that we would have heat even if the power went out.

On that block lived the neighborhood hostess, "JB". She saw to it that there was a "tea" held for each new woman in the neighborhood so that they could get to know their neighbors. I loved the idea and the tea was wonderful. What a genteel bunch of women (mostly natives). "JB" didn't tell me she was an ordained minister until later on in our friend-ship which began with evening walks with our dogs and evolved into chats over hot tea (she was from up north) about our kids and where we had lived and moved, etc. She played a very pivotal part in my life.

When we arrived there we needed jobs. My husband had his, but the children and I needed ones. God provided quickly. My oldest became a house-keeper for a couple down the block with my second child assisting. We also received referrals at the tea for housecleaning and babysitting. So, we all had plenty to do with school, church and work.

My son became a yardman and stall cleaner for the couples' daughter's horses. Evidently cleaning stalls is in the family as my second child cleaned stalls at a horse training academy to pay for her lessons. Additionally, in the season when grass grew (most of the year) all four of us mowed grass on a huge tract of land in a development where the houses weren't built yet and some of which ran along the side of the road for quite a distance. THAT was scary!!!! Sometimes my son's yard work was too much for him alone so we would help. One day I wished I hadn't helped. I was working along pulling weeds out of the ground and as I pulled I suddenly felt a sting, then another and then I went screaming and slapping my legs, arms, neck, etc. Eventually I ran far enough away but as far as my body went I had a bunch of welts and those things burn. I pulled the stingers out and iced them which provided almost no relief. Ibuprofen wasn't much better but it was better than nothing. Evidently I had disturbed a ground nest of yellow jackets. They are the only bees that can sting and sting and sting and not die. I had never heard of bee's nests in the ground. I did NOW.

I also saw my first hornet's nest when we moved here. Those hornets as well as wood boring bees were huge. The wood borers look just like huge bumble bees so I kept my distance from them. Up north I had never seen a hornet. Here, they are plentiful and make huge nests to continue to reproduce and keep the species growing. NO, I did NOT get stung by one of those. But I did get bitten by fire ants, those vicious, hungry tiny red things that make huge red mounds in the grass everywhere which makes it all but impossible to walk on your own lawn or anyone else's for that matter unless you have been unrelenting in treating (killing) them with chemicals. With almost 5 acres of land, it was cost prohibitive to kill them all. All the fun things we did in the grass up north like rolling in it, running barefoot in it, laying out sun tanning on a towel on the grass, all gone because of fire ants. Because if you do make the mistake of stepping in a mound you will not forget you did so. Those bites, each tiny one, blister and drive you out of your mind with itching and then burning and pain. Little kids in particular have a hard time with their bites and sometimes have to go to the doctor for prescription medicine for them.

BIPOLAR ANYONE???

One of the problems I wound up with in my quest for the victorious Christian life was trying to get my doctor to believe in Dissociative Identity Disorder (DID). He believed in the DSM-4 form of DID which is not the same as what I struggle with. *It* calls it a dis-ease, *I* call it a miracle that saved me from dying like my sister did and being completely non-functional like my mom was until she died. It was a miracle that God gave me the ability to split off "parts" or "alters" whichever form you prefer to use to describe it when things were intolerable to a small child who had no escape and couldn't grow up emotionally because of the trauma she experienced.

DID can even begin in the womb if the developing fetus is not wanted by its parents or they had tried to abort it but failed. God allows the developing brain of that person to already split off those painful thoughts and/or experiences in order to protect itself. If acknowledged by the whole mind it could overwhelm it and the child be born developmentally and emotionally flawed.

In my case I had both; parents who didn't want any children and they tried to abort me during my mom's 5th month of pregnancy. Why the 5th month? By that point a woman can neither deny the movement of the child within or the bulging of her abdomen as the child grows. These actions/attitudes by my parents were transferred to my developing brain and God did, indeed, split them off so that I could continue on to be born and to live life. 53 years later God revealed what they had tried to do to me in that 5th month and healed me of the consequences of rejection and self-hatred to name a few and the demons who had been squatting within me had no rights anymore to be there; and they left. I was as shocked as you were about the attempted abortion until I remembered that my grandparents had tried to abort my mother without success also and then I did abort my first child, a girl. This was a family curse in action. The curse is now broken since I confessed, repented, and renounced those actions and lies and affirmed and confessed with my mouth that I believe the truth that Jesus says about life and children. (You were bought at a price therefore glorify God with your body. 1 Cor 6:20)

That sounded pretty neat and exact didn't it? Not at all. In a moment this 54 year old was healed, it was God's timing, not mine. It was 43 years before it was time to begin healing me of all the other horrific abuse I described so far in this book. Healing is messy.

Demons do not like being discovered and their rights to squat within us taken away. They particularly do not like having to leave us and so they made my life miserable in connection with their being evicted, in addition to the regular misery they caused me just by being inside of me. Things like fear, terror, anxiety, fear of death, fear of rejection, fear of punishment, fear of exposure; I could go on for paragraphs about all the demons that were evicted from me but you get the drift. And these are vanilla, every day demons that most of us deal with, sometimes without knowing it. You see, demons want you to think that when they are talking to you that it is you talking to yourself. Good trick until you know the word of God and expose their lies.

When these demons manifest (show themselves by their actions) a person will FEEL like their worst fear is happening even though in reality everything is just fine. Or they will switch so another alter created for this purpose takes on all those feelings. While the alter is doing its job the person may be in the background of his/her mind watching as though in a dream or a movie. When the manifestation is over, the person gets to face the consequences of the demons and alters actions and reactions. Depression and anxiety can set in followed in time by hopelessness, helplessness, and worthlessness; which can lead to suicidal thoughts and actual suicide.

One period during my healing, the pressure of all those demons against me became more than I could handle and I planned my suicide. I did not commit suicide because I kept begging God to save me from myself and He did. I REALLY wanted OUT of this life so my prayer was desperate. Several women of the church prayed with me for hours every day until the desire for suicide passed. Too bad the demons behind the desire for suicide didn't leave. After I finally decided I wanted to live regardless of the pain which was 24/7, the demons ramped up their pressure to convince me that I really did want to commit suicide. They tried several times to finish me off.

One such time was when I was driving down a six lane highway coming home from work and I felt as if something was trying to turn the wheel towards the side of the road. I started praying because the force was strong. It wanted me to destroy myself by running into several cars and the side of the road. It was a fight but Jesus stopped the demons by having me declare that only God can take my life, not them, over and over and over again.

Being unsuccessful in that attempt they tried again one morning to get me to kill myself as I was returning home from college in the car. I had a Joyce Meyer tape playing and I don't recall what she was preaching about but I was thinking about suicide again. I felt that I wasn't going to pass the test I just took inside. I exploded in pain and felt like I couldn't go on. I felt like I would be better off ending it all. Having thought I was finished with the suicide issue I was surprised it surfaced again but I shouldn't have been because this was another part of me who wanted to kill myself. My husband had confessed adultery with two different women just a short time before this and I couldn't deal with the only man I ever trusted having done that to me no matter how many times people told me he was the jerk not me. "DR" and "CR" both said that and "DR" was a Pastor!!!!!

Just as I was going to turn the car into a pole Joyce said on the tape that there was someone struggling with suicide right that very moment. She rebuked the spirit of suicide on the tape and the demonic influence pushing me to kill myself left. I had never experienced God honoring what someone said on a tape meant for an audience at the time working on me. I was astounded. I had trouble believing God loved me so much that He set all that up right up to the moment when I needed to hear from Him most, **after** I told Him that I hated myself, my husband, and my children, that I could never love them again, etc. But I told God that He was bigger than my heart and could change me. (1 Jn 3:20 – Whenever our hearts condemn us ... God is greater than our hearts and He knows everything). Would He? Would he love me even though I was THAT ugly? He sure did and stopped the pain completely. I was so thankful.

I'll admit that I am not the world's fastest learner because even after God showed me again and again what He is capable of doing for me I would still beg God to kill me in order to stop the pain. Months at a time. One particular day I was standing in front of my picture window looking out at the woods of my backyard and I yelled over and over at God: "Will you please kill me?" "Now"?!!! When He said to me: ***"Do you really think that if you scream loud enough I will do it?"*** I couldn't believe that God Himself would speak to me. I mean, God had spoken to me plenty before but never like this!! I would expect to be "smote" but not reasoned with. This confirmed to me again that God existed and cared enough about me to want to answer me. Did it cure my desire to escape my pain? In that alter yes, in the rest of my system, no.

So, I went to the doctor because I cried all the time, didn't want to get out of bed no less out of the house. I was afraid of everyone and everything, I thought people were out to get me, that they hated me. That someone would murder me in my sleep, etc, etc, etc. Other times I was flying high, the sky was extra blue those days; I was scrubbing the kitchen floor at 2 am and buying new clothes even though I had a closet full. One time the professor in my accounting class in college asked me to leave the room because I wouldn't stop calling out. I was so humiliated but I didn't even realize what I was doing. These symptoms happen to match some of those listed in the DSM-4 for Bipolar Disorder; being depressed or down one day or period of time and then becoming superwoman, needing no sleep, feeling invincible, all knowing, fast moving, etc. the next day or period of time.

Because of that I was diagnosed as having Bipolar Disorder II (with depression).When asked if I heard voices, of course I did (my parts) but the doctor said that that made me schizophrenic so I "lost" the voices and stayed just Bipolar!!!!

Why bother to go to the doctor you might ask? To get the medication I needed to lift the depression, stop the manic behavior, to relieve the pain that I had in most of my body which was fibromyalgia; and deal with other medical problems that were the result of all the stress on my body from the mental/emotional problems.

MORE ON DISSOCIATIVE IDENTITY DISORDER

Another of the difficulties of having DID is the denial. DID is a disorder of denial. It has to be because if the original person knew about the alters and felt their pain, they would either go crazy and be hospitalized permanently, or would die. So when God decided it was time to reveal just how I survived my childhood, denial was the premiere feature I saw. Healing could not take place until the alter denial was uncovered and convinced that its job was no longer needed and it voluntarily gave the job to Jesus and rejoined the original person. My alters did not want to cease to exist, they had been inside me for who knows how many years, doing important jobs for me and then suddenly they were no longer needed and were going to be integrated into my original person? Lots of resistance here too, especially for alters who are only equipped with emotion and no cognitive ability, or cognitive but no emotional component; or an alter who was 4 years old and did nothing but cry because she didn't know what was going on. All these issues had to be dealt with in the alter system of the original person before the original person can be made whole. Recently the thinking has changed to not include integration of all alters for the above reasons. They *are* needed. They have done important jobs for the person which the person would not know how to do if they ceased doing their jobs immediately. Once the relationship between the original person and the alters was restored in a way in which everyone was on the same page, the system can function without integration. Alters were valuable and helped me function as the person I was.

The person who was up at the time wound up feeling the feelings of the alters' without any awareness what the problem was. Fear and anxiety seemed to show the most, followed by anger, shame, condemnation, and rage. So there I was in church service on a Sunday morning and all of a sudden I exploded in tears and was so loud that no one in that building would not have heard me. The preacher heard me too and had to preach over all that noise. People would come over to me and wrap themselves around me as I grieved my losses or as God opened me up so that I could see what had been going on inside me. Eventually the crying would stop, sometimes it would last through the entire service and I (the presenting person or person who was up) was humiliated because of the alter's behavior. It was hard to accept and love my alters when their behavior caused me to feel I lost face or was embarrassed or humiliated in front of others. I always felt like the odd one out because of my parts, my alters. DID is caused by intolerable conflict within the person as a result of perceived neglect, trauma, and/or abuse during their childhood and is usually buried until a person's 40's or later, at which time they have teenagers and/or aging parents or both to have to deal with as well. But no matter when the DID begins to surface or why, God does take care of us if we will humble ourselves and ask for His help every time we have a problem of any kind. One thing I should mention is that sometimes there is a gap between our asking God for help and it occurring. It is sometimes a LONG gap but God is faithful to answer us and provide the healing we need.

Then there was the anger, of which I had plenty, that would also explode usually in church during the Sunday Service and at almost every other opportunity like the occasion portrayed in the first chapter of this book. After all I went through as a child I had a seething anger.

In healing, the people working with me had to work with my angry parts (of which there were many because there was so much pain to deal with that one alter could not handle it all). I did not make an "alter map" as others I have heard about, I was too shame ridden to write them down but I can tell you that I had many alters, more than 50 as more than one alter could split out of any one trauma that occurred to cause the splitting in the first place. Only Jesus could heal this pain and cause it to disappear forever. The people working with me were only facilitators, Jesus was the healer. Only He had the authority and power to deal with demons and heal me, and He loved me enough to do it.

Fear was another emotion that was very prevalent and very difficult to get resolved because there was so much of it and because I was labeled a victim. That meant that I had to accept anything thrown at me or done to me because I was a loser, a victim. I couldn't be expected to help myself receive healing, I was helpless. Many victims are programmed (told) by their perpetrators that if they tell anyone what they did to them that they will be killed or that someone in their family will be killed; and they believe it, especially the younger alters.

Upon taking the medicine prescribed for me by my doctor for the Bipolar Disorder there was a curious effect. The voices were less, the depression lifted, the mood swings almost stopped, I was able to sleep an appropriate amount of time each night and felt tired enough to go to sleep. I stopped being tormented by intrusive thoughts and music all the time.

So, was I Bipolar? The medication would say yes because it helped immensely to relieve so much suffering, both physically and emotionally.

Did I kill my parts, my alters? Or medicate them into oblivion? Was this more denial on my part? There were various opinions as to what I did and what I was and it was very painful to live with them because they were so negative and implied that I was not a moral individual, not trustworthy, looking for the easy way out with drugs. Those who thought that way were so sure they were right that I had to fight my way through their opinions to find out what God wanted me to be doing in terms of medicine and DID. I ran into many negative comments regarding DID and, indeed, I wound up taking a stand that resulted in my leaving a church because they no longer believed in DID. I suffered for 3 years because of my opinion about my needing medication AND being DID. I still heard from my alters, just not in an overwhelming frequency and disruptive way, my emotional stability increased with the medications. It seemed to take more to trigger me and the explosions were not quite as severe but I still had them. Having, at that point, had much deliverance and inner healing by a number of Christian methods such as Theophostic Ministry (Ed Smith), Shiloh Place Ministries (Jack Frost), Aslan's Place Ministry (Paul Cox), Elijah House Ministry (John & Paula Sanford), Christian Healing Ministries (Judith & Francis MacNutt), Dr. Grant Mullen, and especially helpful Restoration in Christ Ministry (Tom & Diane Hawkins). WHY wasn't that enough? Why was I still taking these drugs?

Trying to prove that I was healed; I tried at times to go off my medications or even to change them to ones with less negative side effects i.e. the ones that compromise sexual functioning, like inability to have a physical release with my husband during sex, loss of sex drive and loss of sensation. They were the worst side effects. Without my proper medications I wound up crashing so bad that I had to go back on anti-anxiety medications just to deal with the symptoms until the cause was corrected in the brain again.

Still struggling with the truth that God created physical intimacy for us to enjoy you can imagine how I felt one Friday night service where I was doing very poorly during this healing period of time and had stayed in the back of the sanctuary as the service proceeded. It wasn't long before I was down on the floor without benefit of anyone praying for me first. God's glory felt so heavy on me that I couldn't stand up anymore. I was down a while when someone came near me and began singing in tongues. I had no idea who it was, I was face down. It would appear that God wanted to supersede the natural consequences of all my medications and I had what I thought was a spiritual release which felt like the physical release that occurs during physical intimacy. Right on the floor during church service. This was another one of those occasions where the body was way ahead of the brain and by the time my mind understood what was going on with my body and spirit, the shame and feeling that everyone could see and hear what was going on was overwhelming. I had never even entertained the idea that God COULD do such a thing no less that He would WANT to do this for me. My delight turned into wailing, the condemnation came in tidal waves. I had figured out by then who the person was and that made it even worse. I don't think the person knew what was going on with me; just that God was blessing me and then that something happened that changed my delight into terror. The person immediately began praying in English telling Satan in no uncertain terms that he needed to cut out the torture and torment that the person could see was going on. It didn't stop my reaction immediately but I started feeling bad that this poor person was spending all this effort on me so I clamped down and got quiet. Head still buried in my arms on the floor, but quiet. The next time I saw "CR" & "CF". I told them what happened and they informed me that one of them had experienced the same type thing in church previously. She was DID also and we had a lot in common from our childhoods, she was left alone much too young and way too often just like me.

I would, at various times by various people, get told that I just didn't have enough faith. That if I had enough faith I would be healed. It is true that I have heard just recently of people with long standing Bipolar Disease being healed at a Benny Hinn Crusade and during Randy Clark Crusades which my husband and I attended to seek physical healing and have not seen any physical healing manifest since we went to that crusade.

Of course this led to the theological debate about whose fault is it we suffer in our physical bodies. Some teaching I had received said that God was responsible; He was disciplining me and/or developing my character by my suffering. Or that my suffering was so that I could share with Jesus in His glory in heaven when I got there. For most of the last 13 years I believed that. Of course, only if I wasn't healed from whatever suffering I was experiencing at that time, which is another theological view about suffering. Healing and only healing was acceptable to the mature Christian with those beliefs.

And then there is the trial and temptation theory for the origin of human suffering. The bible does speak about trials and temptations. We are tested in our faith to see what we really believe. Of course, God already knows, *we are the ones* that need to see what we really are all about vs. what we think we are all about. Certain knowledge only becomes reality when the person is pushed beyond what they think they can handle; cracks in the faith of the person become evident that would not have been exposed without the pressure of the trial and/or temptation. The bible even goes so far as to say: " Consider it pure joy, my brothers, whenever you face trials of many kinds, because you know that the testing of your faith develops perseverance. Perseverance must finish its work so that you may be mature and complete, not lacking anything." James 1:2-4 .

Then along came the theory that God doesn't cause suffering, it is against His nature. We suffer because we are in a war. A war began by Lucifer when he rebelled in heaven against God and was cast out of heaven with one third of the angels. He was cursed and confined to the earth to contend with men until Jesus returned for the millennial reign. Because of this, Satan hates us and comes to steal, kill, and destroy us with various means (John 10:10 – The thief comes to kill and destroy…). This is illustrated in the bible through JOB. The devil had to ask permission from God to do anything to Job and when he was given a yes, it was a conditional yes, only so far and no further in each instance. God was quite sure Job would survive his suffering and be a better man for it. Satan loses in the end of every story in the bible even if it looks otherwise.

Another theory why those last three years of suffering occurred was that I was being severely pruned. That made sense to me at least. I couldn't understand how painful pruning was and to be honest I had given up any idea that I would be a functional Christian again, used for anything, so bitter and angry. But, as usual, God healed all the pain and anger and bitterness and at the same time increased my faith in Him. It was Christians who attacked me and it was Christians who brought restoration to me despite my wanting nothing to do with even those Christians that I knew for many years and were close friends. (Psalm 41:9 – Even my close friends whom I trusted, he who shared my bread has lifted up his heel against me).

It was part of the price I paid for following Jesus and trying to do His will, but nothing like the ultimate price Jesus paid for me to forgive those who hurt me so badly. At that point, vulnerability and trust were elusive both in my marriage and in my relationships with other Christians. I am willing to receive more healing, if that is what Jesus wants, but at least I can live peacefully at this point. The Lord has restored our capacity as prayer ministers and has seen fit to send people to us for healing and deliverance again for which I am so thankful.

By now you can see how the various traumas in my childhood and young adult life created an individual whose soul was shattered into many pieces which were represented by an alter system. Because of this alter system things happened in my life that looked completely opposite of what I had previously done or said. This was because another part of me, one of my core parts or an alter part was making the decision at that particular moment and her decision had to do with how she felt and what she knew about the world that "The team" lived in all those years. This was played out in church as our family went from being Lutheran to being Assembly of God, to being Southern Baptist to being Assembly of God to Independent Baptist to Presbyterian and finally to being Nondenominational believing in the "full gospel" that Pentecostals confess. Of course, at the time my family did not understand what was going on with me, but neither did I so we were even. I felt I was hearing from God to keep switching churches over disagreements with doctrine on how conservative a life we were to live. I kept swinging from liberal to conservative to very conservative to less conservative etc. My kids were angry because they couldn't make friends as we never stayed put in a church long enough for them to do so except when they were very young. This also made them dump the whole "organized religion" thing, kind of like throwing out the baby with the bathwater. I tried to explain to them that the precepts were the same in each church; i.e. Jesus as Savior, God the one and only Father and the Holy Spirit where the power comes from to believe on Jesus and have Him pay for your sins so that you can get into heaven. We didn't go from Christians to Buddhists to Hindus to Hare Krishnas, etc. etc. but they didn't care. It was something they could use to rebel and rebel they did.

During that time of rebellion for them I began having panic attacks in church. I would try to sing and praise and pray and many times I was not able to enter into God's presence. I now know that was because I had an alter (or more than 1) up (conscious) and they didn't believe all this Jesus stuff and would rather have been anywhere but church. I will refer to the time period that we were "spirit filled" Presbyterians during this chapter. When service was over each Sunday or Friday night there would be people up front who would pray for people who needed prayer. My husband and I served on this rotation as well. Many of the times the power of God and His glory would come so strongly that people (including me) would "fall out" in the Spirit and wind up being caught by another person and let down to rest on the carpet. God did tremendous amounts of work in people as they did what we called "carpet time". I found out recently that even the Baptists did carpet time back in history but not anymore today. What would the person feel who was doing carpet time? Any of a combination of a deep abiding peace which washed away the anxiety that the world inflicted on them between services, to hysterical laughing as though everything is funny (that was the JOY of the Lord manifesting on the people) to hysterical crying as God opened a wound the person may or may not had known he/she had and God decided it was time to deal with it and bring the person healing. Sometimes demons would manifest. Their job was to humiliate the person who was resting on the carpet by putting on a negative show like that. Usually people in the prayer teams had been trained to deal with demon manifestations so they started doing so the minute they saw the manifestation. The demons didn't always leave right then, sometimes they were bound by the prayer ministers to await being ejected in a more private, intensive setting by appointment. Doing it by appointment meant that there was a thorough discovery of how much and what type demonization a person had which led to complete freedom from evil spirits in that session. Sometimes nothing would leave. Not to worry, it just meant that they still had legal grounds to be squatters in the person in question seeking deliverance.

Many times I would not want to go to church because I was angry or sad but I would not let that stop me from asking God to change my mind about going. People could deal with whatever I wound up doing in the church service. One usual Sunday I arrived at church and worship began and I was singing along. The next thing I know I was hit with a torrent of negative feelings. Where was this coming from I wanted to know? I was fine a minute ago. Answer: God knew I had junk inside that I was trying to run from in my head by switching to another alter who didn't have the issue making me explode emotionally. I called these moments fondly: God's divine can opener. The alter that rose up to handle being happy and sweet pushed off all the pain and ugliness to another alter in the system who was so very tired of being dumped on. And finally she had had enough and there came the torrential uproar of negative emotions. Most alters have to deal with the negative emotions and behavior that the "good Christian" that we believed we were could exist and act like that good Christian. That was why alters remained hidden inside the system and took much working with them for them to decide that they were willing to have a new job for Jesus inside the person. The person may react with tremendous denial because, after all, that was why they split the alters off in the first place, because they were a danger to the system of the individual. "I" just had to wait it out until Jesus came and took the pain and ugliness away from that alter so that the rest of me could praise and pray and be in God's presence.

FIRST HEALING OF THE MEMORIES

As I have mentioned, I spent 5 years in counseling with "DR". What follows is from my journal for that period of time, detailing my first "healing of the memories" and some of those that followed.

As my time with the counseling pastor began, I spent two hours talking about the most uncomfortable things for me. I was surprised how easily it went. I KNEW it was prayer that was making the difference or I would not have been able to do it. We went on to the healing of the memory experience about that man who exposed himself to me when I was young. "DR" wondered why I reacted to that experience with revulsion instead of curiosity. I couldn't tell him why I reacted that way. I told him that I had the feeling that I was forgetting something. He said that we would just ask Jesus as we were doing the healing of the memory and that He would tell us the missing information. I guess I was kind of skeptical about that, but I knew we needed to continue. We did work through the memory and this time I had more feelings and tears and when I asked Jesus why I perceived the experience with revulsion instead of curiosity there was a tense silence. Right about when I was about to give up came the words: Because your father had a penis. I was like WHAT??? God revealed that I had a preconceived idea that penises were my sworn enemies because as I was developing years before, my uncle and father had a pastime of looking through my nightgowns and I got chewed out and called names because I didn't know any better than to wear them without a robe because they were almost see through. Add that to the incident with my father wanting me to sit on his lap and I was afraid they would molest me. I had also learned the anatomical facts of sex from a "Family Health Encyclopedia" hidden in a closet in my childhood home and it sounded gross and painful to me and the drawings were ugly and frightening too. That big thing in that little space? No Way. That was why penises were my sworn enemy. Jesus was there in the memory and he took me in His arms and told me that I wasn't a slut, degraded and worthless, that I was just a girl looking for love and acceptance that I didn't understand how to get. He told me I was safe, and that I wouldn't become a lesbian (another of my fears) because men were my enemies. At that time I had a very poor understanding of women who were lesbians and thus was afraid of them. It was a good experience with Jesus. I had been afraid to try this memory healing method but it was no where as bad as I thought it would be. Jesus was gentle with me.

There were no demons attached to that memory but I had my first attempt at deliverance shortly thereafter. Also, my having DID wasn't discovered until the second year in counseling.

"DR" had said that we needed to do a healing for the memory of my second child's reaction to my past and I balked from fear. A few weeks earlier "DR" identified another memory that I needed to do concerning fear of humiliation. This memory God revealed to me a month before this date with the same response from me – NO. I had wondered if my problem had not been with the demons, but my refusal to trust God to heal me. I hadn't realized that I wasn't going forward with the healing of the memories because I was afraid God would let me down; that I would try to do it and get nothing. I didn't realize I was trying to protect myself from failure by being afraid. "DR" had said in Sunday school two weeks prior that we use FEAR to protect ourselves and that was wrong. God must be our protector, through discernment by His Spirit. It was a marvelous experience, unlike any of the others we had done before. When we began, I could not get a clear picture of what I was wearing back then. I said I was wearing shorts and a white top. "EG" was only wearing a bra (I knew there was a shirt over it, but I couldn't see anything.) But her face was there and her voice came booming through and so did the volcano of pain and tears. "DR" said that the reason I couldn't see her clothes was that I was afraid of her. I told him I could feel the hate, anger, condemnation, rejection, worthlessness and judgment coming from her. When he said to push the pain out of me into Jesus I thought I was. Then I felt that I wasn't chest to chest with Him, but rather side to chest. I didn't think it made any difference. "DR" said that that was a lot of pain to push out, a big wound. He told me to remember that this child was the only one I thought understood me and supported me during the previous 6 months when we first started going as a family to that church. God just took me through the things that were hurting me. Shame, failure, having ruined her life with something I did 20 years ago; were all given to Jesus. He reassured me of His love and acceptance. "DR" had me ask Jesus if "EG" and I would ever have a relationship again. I suddenly had a picture of myself, "EG" and a year old baby riding on a merry-go-round. I started wailing again because I figured this must be 10 years down the road and I didn't want to wait that long for her to love me again. "DR" reassured me that this was just a reassurance from God that I would have this in the future, but not necessarily that it would take that long to get there. Then, without my even asking, God spoke to me about my feeling of being defective. This had been coming up lately, and after the shame issue, was the biggest problem I think I had. God told me that **I WAS NOT DEFECTIVE.** I had some defects, namely, wounds. The wounds were like broken parts. God showed me that I was like a watch that had broken parts. A watch that had been dropped by no fault of its own and now was not keeping time rightly, all the time. Sometimes it did, but sometimes it didn't. The watchmaker needed to repair the broken parts so that the watch would run correctly again. God was healing my wounds which were the broken parts of my heart. "DR" got all choked up and said he was sorry for never telling me that. I was in shock with joy over God telling me this. I had not even asked. I was laughing and crying at the same time. "DR"'s next appointment had arrived so we had to end but not before I told Jesus thank you. We went back to that memory one more time and this time I saw "EG" yelling at me and I just started laughing. He hoped I didn't do that in real life!! (I wouldn't). I wound up saturated with God's love and anointing so I went in the room next door and laid down a while until I could stand up again to drive home.

Shortly after that memory healing I had another deliverance appointment where nothing was manifesting and nothing was leaving either. It was "DR", "CR" and the pastor who works with the youth, "AMK" in addition to working on the deliverance team, who was working with me. Just when I was getting very discouraged God gave "CR" and I a vision at the same time. I started to feel like I was being shaken even though my body wasn't moving. As I told this to "CR", she and I saw the TV comedy man being held upside down and shaken until his stolen goods fell out of his pockets. This was how my father had operated. He stole from the government and anyone else he could. "CR" said that I needed to renounce my inheritance and agree not to take a penny of it if it was cursed (because of my dad's stealing it). I told her that would be hard and she said I better get with it. I told her to wait a minute while God gave me the grace to do it. We laughed. I did renounce it. Then someone made a comment which I felt stupid about and the tears came. So did deliverance: scapegoat, screaming banshee(s), blame, reproach, incompetence, and others I can't remember. I was so thankful. I wound up hurting physically, spiritually and emotionally as those demons tore me up as they left. By the time that "CR" realized that that was what the pain was, some had already completed their damage. I finally felt better on the 4th day after the deliverance appointment.

That same day I received a notice from the kids' school that my second child was beyond her 5 absence limit for the semester. I KNEW that she had had only 3 days off with my dad's funeral so I called and they said the other 4 days were accompanied by a note signed by her father!!!! My husband never signs notes, his writing is illegible. The days were Mondays and Fridays directly after she had turned 17 and was assured by her older new friends that the Police would not force her to return home if she chose to leave. By the time I got off the phone I was so hysterical that even after "CR" praying for me there was too much pain to deal with. She asked me if I could go see Jesus in the park? I had had a healing of the memories only a few days before concerning a birthday party that I forced my way into being invited, and then was spurned and humiliated by the girls there. When I found Jesus, he was at the park near my house. He told me that He was my forever friend and that I would never be alone again. I told "CR" yes and I laid down on the floor and howled and kicked my feet and cried like I thought I would never stop for 30 minutes. It was a really different cry. And then God told me to go put a CD on with praise on it. I listened to it and then praised Him anyway. The 5th song on that disc was about grief and how Jesus was with us in the valley of grief. How He blessed us forever and how we were His forever. I was so blessed. I went to my 12 step meeting that night and gave a glowing testimony of how God met me in my need. I was grieving. Grieving the loss of the child I thought I had raised because the one that I had now wasn't them and an alien took over their body somehow!!!! But God took all the pain.

It was time for another deliverance appointment. "CR" and "CF" spent two hours with me getting nowhere. There was only a little time left before I had to go to work and I was starting to worry that I would leave without having gotten rid of any pests when God told "CF" to put her fingers in my ears. She was kind of wondering how I was going to take it, but she obeyed. "CR" had her hands on the side of my head. Suddenly I was back in the pool with the next door neighbor as he almost drowns me. I told "CR" to stop and I told her what I was feeling and I grabbed hold of her and wailed. She prayed for inner healing of that memory and then for deliverance of fear of suffocation and fear of strangulation. I saw my mother and her brother in the spirit and sensed that it was generational, maybe even a curse. We did the witchcraft renouncements and then continued with the deliverance. "CR" went after every demon that could have come in through the near drowning and it was interesting how when she named the right demon I would wince and try to hide (that was the demons wincing and trying to hide). But leave they did and I was glad. I had asked a couple of women to pray that this time I wouldn't rip or tear as the demons left and God honored that.

I had to go for a repeat lab test at the ob-gyn's one day and the test turned out fine but my blood pressure was way up. I was shocked. Then I had to get on the scale and I found I had gained back everything I had recently lost on my new diet. All in the last 4-5 months. I made it out of the office and to the car when the dam broke. I was in so much pain. I just cried and cried and cried. I called out to God to help me, help me, help me. I wasn't going to be able to work and I was on the way there. I told God that if He didn't want me to work it was ok; I would yield to His plan. I heard him say to me that **I was only 8 years old emotionally** and that wasn't old enough to take care of all the things that had been happening to me. HE WILL take care of me. It's OK with HIM if I can't. When I heard that, it was all over. I was fine, the pain was gone. Somehow a child alter wound up being conscious for this appointment and I didn't know it until afterward but God took care of me like He always does.

Another day when I was meeting with "DR" I knew that we were scheduled for another healing of the memories. As the time was ticking away, interrupted by phone calls and other disturbances, the anxiety rose within me. Finally there was only 15 minutes left and I had made the assumption that there wasn't enough time left to do the healing.

I was wrong. "DR" said that the only responsibility I had was to ask God which memory and once God brought it up that it was HIS problem what happened when I went back into it. I told him that I was having difficulty remembering details which I knew he would be asking me for. He told me that I wasn't in the memory yet. I was skeptical to put it mildly at that point when "DR" began with having me imagine diving into my little person's head. It was so exciting when "DR" had me look down at my legs and there were the coral shorts with the button over my waist that I wore when I was a teenager!! The white V neck tank top was on me too. As he had me look around my room, my white French provincial furniture was there too. I don't think I even own a PHOTO of that furniture. God was providing the memory to me. It was hard for me to say to "DR" that my "FH" was sitting against the door and I was lying up against him and he had one hand on my breast and the other "down there" but I said it. I was enjoying what "FH" was doing. As I heard my father coming up the stairs we struggled to close up and straighten up. I could hear my father put the grocery bags on the table and his change on the dryer. He walked right past my door and continued down into his bedroom. My "FH" opened my bedroom door and walked around the table and out the door to the stairs going outside. I stood in the doorway and my father came down the hall (I was waiting to see what he would say because I had no memory of words). He just looked at me and then walked away. I was already overheated and flushed from activity, now I was red from shame. I went back into my room and stood facing the closet. "DR" asked me what I was feeling. Originally I was panicking from fear of being discovered, fear of punishment and humiliation, fear of rejection, helplessness, powerlessness, shame of being discovered, and now I WAS ANGRY. I was surprised to find anger in this memory. I had to ask God what the anger was from. It was from my father giving me that "you slut" wilting look when at the same time he was banging his girlfriend and it was ok for him but not for me. I couldn't believe what I was discovering. I was angry at my "FH" for abandoning me by running out and leaving me to face my father alone.

"DR" asked me to turn around (in my mind) and see who was there. It was Jesus. He was motioning to me with His hand to come to HIM. I went running and jumped into HIS arms and when I did, I was hit with such a powerful anointing that I was shocked. "DR" told me to squeeze all the pain into Jesus and squeeze out all the anger, shame and humiliation and as I did I was jolted again. By now I was crying and leaning forward. "DR" told me to let go of Jesus with one arm and look at HIM. He was crying. HE had tears in HIS eyes. "DR" asked WHY? I said because Jesus was sad that I was hurting. Then he had me ask Jesus questions. Why did my "FH" run out? He ran because he was afraid that if he remained my father would ask him questions that he couldn't lie about and that those answers would cause my father to forbid my "FH" to see me anymore. My "FH" loved me and didn't want to lose me so he left. Why did my father act like he did? Jesus answered: he didn't know any better. He had teenage girls that he was clueless to raise. His best friend's daughter got pregnant and he didn't want that to happen to me. He had to answer to my Aunt about what I was doing. Somehow, in that warped mind of his, he cared. Was it ok for me to feel what I did? Jesus said yes, that he made my body the way it was and it was ok. Will I ever have anything like that with my husband? Yes, I will, I'm free. I got hit again with the anointing power of the presence of God through the Holy Spirit.

I started crying again and asked God to take the pain. "DR" asked what I wanted to do now. I told him that I wanted to thank Jesus for helping me. He said to give Jesus a thank you hug. I did. I felt so much love, like Jesus would never leave me and would always be there for me. "DR" said it was time to come back from the memory and I said NO WAY, I don't want to come back. I had, by then, bent over to the side of the couch to rest and sat up and opened my eyes. "DR" asked if Mona was such a bad person. Mona was the alter that was split off to have sex because I was bad if I had sex so I had to give the task to an alter or several. Mona was NOT a bad person, intimacy is a gift from God and I didn't have to feel dirty because I liked it. Once I can own my right to have and enjoy sex, Mona should integrate back into me and I'd be whole again. It didn't happen that day.

I realized as Jesus healed the memory that the look my father gave me violated my boundaries and caused me shame. I never had any boundaries and that is why I felt so much shame. God said that He was going to rebuild my boundaries so that I was not violated that way anymore. He also covered me with His robe again at the end of the memory to cover my shame and vulnerability. It was wonderful. "DR" prayed that I would be drunk all night once I got home. Each time I would think about what Jesus did I would be touched by His power again. It was a challenge to drive home, but I did fine because God drove the car again.

After that healing of the memories there was plenty of sex. I don't know if it was Miss Mona or another part but whoever it was had a big need and capacity for sex. The first couple of times were like "YES, I AM A WOMAN AND IT IS GOD'S DESIGN THAT I HAVE THIS PHYSICAL RELEASE!!" Isn't it wonderful? Then the struggle began again and things were going no where, but I wasn't about to give up. Just as I hit the no return point my husband started praying in tongues and I was just about catapulted through the ceiling. The explosion and ensuing tidal wave of pleasure was such a shock/surprise that I completely lost control for the next several minutes. It was glorious. I then remembered what it was like 13 months previously. There was such a peace, a fulfillment, a contentment, a "let the world go on without me, I'm having too much fun here" type thing. Such abandon, yes, that was the word. I even saw Jesus at the end of the bed looking on and smiling. Yes, that was what He intended and why he made sex for married couples. After I saw Jesus at the bottom of the bed the shame that I struggled with was gone.

As if that wasn't enough, the next day (that was 4 days running) I was sitting there listening to Chuck Swindoll on the internet and my husband comes home from work. I had been "daydreaming about sex all day at work" and when he bent over to kiss me hello, I got hit with a major dose of anointing and doubled over the computer. I looked at my husband and he looked at me and I wound up desperately trying to find a place to get ravaged right there by the computer. It was incredible. Every cell/nerve in my body was ignited. It got to the point where I was mad that humans wear so MANY clothes as I struggled to rip mine off and his too. Then, nothing, both of us on the couch and ....oh, well. Get redressed and continue on with the day.

The next day we went to see a movie, The General's Daughter. It was a sad movie in that the woman was a dominatrix who hated men because her father had molested her when she was young. My husband had wanted sex again and I wanted to be in Nome, Alaska. But I remembered how good it had been the other day and wanted that again, so even though I didn't feel like I could I wanted to anyway. I didn't have any emotional involvement at all. It was just physical. The physical felt good but once again no release. I hated that and I wasn't about to give up. I tried all the usual fantasies and nothing worked until I saw the porn scene in the above movie where the general's daughter was humiliated during sex that she didn't know was being recorded. The desired release was accomplished along with the shame that I felt because the only way I could give my husband what he wanted was by viewing porn again. She gets killed in the movie by one of her johns. Her father would never take responsibility for what he did to her in childhood either. I wound up getting hysterical after my husband asked me if I was ok. He immediately began binding the demons as I explained why I felt exposed and humiliated just by telling him what went on just then. I asked him if he wanted to be married to a pervert and he said it was fine with him but that that wasn't me; it was a separated part whose job it was to have sex with him. I wished that I would be completely healed in that area because many times when I was able to connect emotionally I wound up with what sounds like a spring that suddenly lost compression and pops, revealing intense fear of abandonment among other negative feelings.

THE PLAYBOY BUNNY
AND CHURCH

One of my parts wanted to be a Playboy Bunny. She decided to make an appearance in church one Sunday morning and there were the ingredients for an explosion. I couldn't worship. I was trying to talk to myself and trying to stay calm. I was blocked. The pressure began to build but I didn't understand that that was what was happening. At the end of the last song of the worship set God popped the lid and out came all the pain, the disappointment, the hope-lessness, despair, etc. God reminded me that He was with me when life was very hard and He brought me through it. He would get me through this too. That gave me hope and I was able to settle down during the rest of the service. At the end of service I went up for prayer and while I was down on the carpet my husband came over to pray for me. He said that he understood what my Playboy bunny part was going through; that she couldn't understand what was wrong with showing a beautiful body. My husband said that it caused lust and that was bad. For her it was a heart thing; wanting to be loved, valued, taken care of, admired, and seen as special. NOT a sex thing. She didn't understand why we had to have sex anyway. All it did was mess things up. It caused men to be animals and women to be used, hurt, needy, embarrassed when they can't have sex and condemned because they wanted to. It's not that she wanted other men to see her naked. She was thinking about how she wanted to be beautiful naked, not ugly, fat, scarred, flabby, too short, fat waisted, etc, etc. As a bunny she would be important, valuable, and special. Men would want to treat her special, take care of her, etc. My husband then wanted to show her how much he loved her and everything was fine until it was time to get undressed. Then, poof, she was gone. After much prayer and work on his part there was a release but I didn't feel it. He said that that was alright because he had prayed that whichever of my parts needed it received it and that was what was important. The rest of the night was war inside. The demons were on the warpath pounding me with one or another form of torment. My husband would pray and bind them and I wouldn't get any relief. He would pray some more and bind some more and I would get relief for a little while. Then the physical began; the onslaught of shooting pains down both of my legs again. He got mad and prayed in tongues aggressively. He told God that he wanted me FIXED and was frustrated because I wasn't getting fixed. I couldn't see Jesus, hear Jesus, or anything and that frustrated both of us. I did finally get relief from the pain as I fell asleep.

It was hard because I couldn't understand what was going on but I remember thinking that this was hard but I'd make it. I'd made it so far. I made it that time because Jesus was still Jesus and He was how I made it.

One other day, I was leaving to do schoolwork when my husband asked me where I was going. I told him and he asked me if I wanted a back rub first. I said, of course, because my back had been hurting lately. I was feeling emotionally needy and my husband responded with lovemaking. I was frightened since the last time was such a nightmare. He asked me what was going on and I told him the truth. He said that it was fine if we just kissed so that I could get my emotional needs met. We were touching full skin, which satisfied that need, but I wanted more and so he cooperated. I could feel the switch take place from Ms. Vulnerable and Needy to some protector alter. I tried talking to the protector with no result that I could tell but I wasn't going to stop my husband from enjoying it. He said he would stop, that he wanted to give to me and didn't need anything for himself, but I said no, that I would feel good if I could see that I pleased him. It was my job to please him and most of the time I couldn't even do that right.

After he was done I asked him to take care of me. The only way that I could get the release I needed was to pretend he was a mechanical sex toy. I remembered an article I read about frigidity and the author's advice to get a good mechanical sex toy and then talk about who is frigid. Once I imagined that that was what it was, bango! I can see where she is coming from (pun!). No emotional involvement, just a machine. I could sense that this protector didn't want my husband to see her enjoy herself as if it was bad and he would laugh or worse yet, use sex as a means to manipulate her because she was needy. I was so happy that God revealed what she was thinking and what her issues were. I told my husband about it and he wasn't offended. He said that now he looks at this stuff not as rejection, but as God working to heal me. I felt closer to him because of it and I really needed that release. I think I was walking around with a lot of physical tension because of the several botched attempts at release over those last two weeks.

We soon attempted physical intimacy again and I had another little person (alter) surface. I was **not** thrilled at this turn of events but I guess I'm more healed than before because I was able to deal with it without a riot. Actually, I think that more than one alter was up because originally I was afraid to even try. I kept hearing that I should ask my husband to pray, that WE should pray before we attempted the act, but I resisted because I felt like it was dirty and that I couldn't ask GOD to bless animal lust. Like I wish God wouldn't watch, like I want to HIDE this activity from God. My husband sensed that I wasn't "there" and asked me and I told him with much hesitance what I was hearing. He had no problem with that and he prayed. Nothing. He asked Jesus whether he should minister to whoever was up or if Jesus would please put someone up who could participate in this activity. He didn't hear that he was to minister to whoever was up and yet he did minister by not pushing her to someplace she couldn't handle. As I was lying there I believe that God answered my husband's request as I became interested in what he was suggesting and was thinking how wonderful it was to be able to have that release and have a man touch my usually covered up body. Before we began, my husband put his hand in my underwear and the response was amazing, AND THEN I heard "he's got his hand in my underwear"!!!! And THAT as they say, was the END of the story. It took me a few minutes to realize what happened (God gave me the revelation) that immediately upon hearing from this separated part, the religious protector shut everything down and issued shame and condemnation to me. God told my husband that at that point to go ahead for himself and shortly thereafter it was over. But, not liking to be "left at the altar" my husband tried to help me. Even though I understood that I was not BAD, but had a little person who *felt* bad, nothing happened. I finally asked my husband to stop because I was afraid of getting still another clogged pore/infection in the labia and/or another yeast infection which I am prone to.

I felt anger, worthlessness, resentment, rejection, disappointment, confusion, self betrayal, self hatred, self loathing and fear of retaliation as I got up, and shame again because I didn't function like a normal woman, the "freak" thing again. I realized that there was blame shifting going on inside as someone tried to blame my husband for having ruined me at 15 by having this kind of physical contact. That was 30 years ago and we were CHILDREN who (looking back) were lucky they could even do simple things no less get involved in sex. I was just as much responsible because I wanted it also, so I can't blame him. I was sitting there typing and wishing that sex didn't exist. It was not worth the trouble. I can't complain actually because I had had some decent sex in that last couple of weeks, it was just hard to be reminded I'm a failure again by what had happened. I was thinking that that COULDN'T be because I had the most powerful healing of the memories EVER on this very issue (although not the exact same incident, this one was at the movies which I can't even imagine I did, I certainly have no memory of it). I felt like somehow I was hopeless because I didn't get healed like I just said because look at what happened that day again. I tried talking to this part later once I realized what was going on. It was hard because I didn't want to have that problem, she brought me shame, but I realized that if this WAS what was going on that it was better for me to love her. She wanted to go to the usual porn sites in my mind in order to finally have the physical release, but I wasn't going there. I'd rather walk around sore and frustrated than do that again. I even tried, after saying I wouldn't, to go to those mental sites, but nothing worked which made the shame even worse. I needed to have that physical release to prove I could. I guess I get a lot of my worth from my ability to perform sexually. And now I could add the word hypocrite to my resume.

I think it is worth mentioning again that I sinned a lot during this healing period. My reaction to being cleaned up, refined, polished, fired in the oven, etc. etc. was anger, resentment, bitterness, betrayal, injustice, desire for revenge, pride, violation and failure and yet God understood and blessed me anyway as in the following example of a Sunday morning service.

Worship began and I cried with thankfulness as God's spirit surrounded and encompassed my entire being. So much love, acceptance, peace, and joy that I was wiped out, with total continuous saturation. It had really begun in Sunday school when the person teaching the class told us that God talked to the angels about US (me and my separated parts). At that point I just lost it. The anointing hit me and I was leveled all the way down to my toes I think. SUCH GREAT LOVE for me after ALL I'd done. Standing there screaming, cursing, stomping up and down for hours in front of the church door the previous Wednesday night bible study and with all the other times here and there with the same rage reaction and He tells the angels about ME? Of course, yes, He had FORGOTTEN all about that, I just had a bad day and he UNDERSTOOD that this happened to me every so often. He was NEVER disappointed in me because He already knew what I was going to do. It was FORGIVEN and then FORGOTTEN. SUCH FREEDOM!!!!

MORE ON THE ABORTION

Continuing on with my healing came the healing of the memory of the abortion. My husband didn't come with me to the abortion procedure; it was the day after we returned from our honeymoon and opening day of hunting season. I wound up throwing up all afternoon (I realized later that the vomiting was from nerves). In order to do the abortion they needed to get into the cervix and because I had never had a child it was completely closed. They administered a shot to the cervix so they would then dilate it manually (that shot hurt like forever). As they began the procedure I could hear the vacuum machine running and causing me to cramp everywhere it touched. It actually only took a few minutes to complete the procedure. "DR" had me picture the examination table that I was on as he began the healing of the memory. God had told him to start the healing right after everyone left me alone in that room after the procedure and that was what we did. It was a still photo, not a moving one. I tried to talk but couldn't, I had just murdered my baby. Two lone tears escaped my eyes. "DR" asked me how I felt about it and I told him I didn't want to have done that. "DR" said to me to stop stuffing my emotions at which time I began screaming Angela, Angela, Angela (that was the name I gave her). Tears were now running down my face as the pain surfaced. The next scene I had was back at the apartment where I was all alone. "DR" asked me what I was feeling and I told him that I was struggling with the whole thing. He said not to be afraid, just let him lead me. I said fine. He started by asking me about why I was alone and told me if I would just look over the side of the bed on the other side of the room, someone was there. I looked and there was Jesus with his arms out. It felt like an old trusted friend was there and we were going to catch up on life. I went over and hugged Him. "DR" told me to press out my pain into Jesus and I did. I did not feel the overwhelming relief that I did with the last memory healing that we did. I did feel my legs and torso relax and loosen from the contorted way I was sitting. I felt peace. "DR" continued to list feelings I should have been feeling but for some reason wasn't. Anger, guilt, hypocrisy, stupidity, condemnation, worthlessness, uselessness, humiliation, rejection, fear of retaliation, fear of abandonment, fear of punishment, fear of exposure, self hatred, self loathing, failure and shame. He had me ask Jesus if He would take those feelings even though I wasn't able to get in touch with them. Jesus said He would and I asked Him to do it. "DR" had me ask Jesus about the abandonment from my husband, about the sex issue (this is all sex is about, pain, shame, guilt, anger). Jesus said that that wasn't what sex was about. Satan used sex to try to destroy me and my marriage. I asked Jesus why my husband didn't come with me to the abortion procedure and the answer was because my husband was ashamed of himself and what he did to me. "DR" didn't think that was the answer and so he asked me if I was SURE that was what Jesus was saying. I asked Jesus to show me if there was another answer and if this was just my flesh answering instead of God and I didn't hear any other answers. "DR" got up and gave me some tissues because my shirt was getting all wet and I hadn't bothered to get any tissues. The healing was over and "DR" asked me to come back. I asked Jesus one more question. Did we do this?, and He said yes. I was not able to connect with my feelings and was concerned that because of that that it wasn't real. God showed me the picture of a camera iris closing the opening of light and said that this was the wound being closed by God's healing of my heart. This was what was needed, the healing of the wound. No more legal grounds for demons. I really think that a lot of the pain was healed years ago when my spiritual mother "EG" and I went through the abortion counseling/healing during which I named Angela. As I was leaving, "DR" asked me if I was OK. I told him that God did what God wanted to do in there and that was OK. I drove home and was feeling uneasy. I started to type my journal and realized that I needed to call my husband and have him come home to be with me (it was past 6 pm already). I called him and he said he would come home. I didn't ask him to pray, but I should have. I laid down on the couch and just started praying and asking Jesus to comfort me and show me if I needed to do anything else. I just sensed His peace and I guess I fell asleep for a few minutes. I guess something was blocking or masquerading as blocking what God was doing in there because as I was typing this "DR's" words "Don't stuff" rang in my ears and I felt God's anointing falling on me. I believe it is worth mentioning that I received this healing despite previous occasions and methods of healing used to heal the wound of the abortion. I think that this was a separated part, an alter, that still had this pain and that she was made clean when this healing of the memories took place. When things happened to me they affected my whole system (I didn't even know it) and so healing must come to the whole system and this was a part of it.

PANIC AT PRAYER MEETING

On Saturday nights my husband and I would attend the revival prayer meetings at church. During one of these prayer meetings the head of the worship team was praying about getting cleaned up, being pure before God, not hiding secret sins in our heart, being willing to allow God to cut through the denial in us to admit we have problems that we won't deal with. I wound up with rage in a skinny minute. Did he have any clue what he was talking about? How dare he pray such a thing? I hated all this cleaning up, I hated never knowing when the next ugly, wicked sinful attitude, thought, idea, word or action would break forth out of me and believe me they do because here we were again in church and I was in a rage.

Panic hit next and try as hard as I could, I could NOT bring it down. Nothing I prayed did a thing. I felt tremendous shame, guilt, condemnation, fear of punishment, etc. I had disrupted and indeed, stopped their prayer time. I might have shocked and scared several of the people there (one of which was a doctor). I was beet red from the top of my head down into my chest and it was very visible to those around me even though I had pulled my jacket over my head and had my head way down between my knees. I didn't understand what was happening to me. First my husband (who knew what it was), then the youth pastor were praying for me with their hand on my back and head. I just got worse and wished I could have disappeared through the floor. I wanted to run, but couldn't move. I had been feeling so hopeless only a few minutes previously because I hadn't believed Jesus existed no less wanted to help me. I was sure He was mad at me because I was being so ungrateful and angry about my situation. Then "DR" came over to me and started saying things like: "Jesus loves you, can you go to Him?" To which I answered I'm SO angry. He said that Jesus knew that and that Jesus loved me even though I was angry. Jesus knew the anger was coming from pain in my heart. I told him He was right. I had already asked Jesus several times to take the pain and anger but "DR" said to ask Him yet again. "DR" said to go to Jesus and He wouldn't hurt me because He already knew why I was the way I was and it was ok with Him. I asked Jesus if He would protect me (I was thinking about people who wanted to hurt me, use me, humiliate me, etc.) and Jesus said He would. I didn't understand why a few minutes ago I hadn't even believed Jesus could have existed and yet now I could see Him sitting there and I went and climbed up in his lap and put my head on His chest. With great racking sobs I held on for dear life and let Him love me. Poor "DR", on his knees next to me asked if he could get up because of his knees and I said I was sorry that his knees hurt. I curled up on my husband's lap and "DR" threw a jacket over me so that I could have some privacy. I still wept, but with a combination of relief and gratitude because GOD DOES KNOW ME. (At least one alter was up during this revelation with Jesus. A child who didn't understand anything except she was bad and a protector alter whose job it was to hide the little one so that she couldn't be hurt anymore. The Protector was asked to give up her job and join the whole person at a later date). I was clueless about what happened to me and so embarrassed; and yet God chose this time to show me He could fix me without my even knowing what was going on. It WAS humbling and awe inspiring at the same time. It seemed to me that there wasn't much prayer after that. In a few minutes prayer was over. I was ok.

The next day at service I had asked God to enable me to worship Him and so I waited for Him to give it to me. I felt nothing. I could not sing, not open my mouth, or lift my hands, nothing. I wondered what it was all about. I was feeling that everyone was condemning me for not praising, not worshipping but I knew that my relationship with Jesus was not one of works, it was one of my heart and I wanted Him in my heart. I could see my little people in their room in my mind. Praising Jesus and I could hear them inside, but nothing moved on the outside of me. I felt so exposed again, I wanted to leave. I guess what I did by now praising was to give myself privacy the only way I could. I always felt exposed and violated during church services. I felt God's anointing hit me that day and I buckled. I stood back straight and thought "someone up there has my number, knows where I am". The next song went by and I felt it again with the same reaction in my body. I wondered why God would do that. The next song was Draw Me Close to you, (never let me go, I need the warmth of your embrace...) And I broke. Gaping sobs and wracking pain. About that time I heard a commotion and glanced to see the pastor's son blubbering and telling his father who was now in front of him "I love you". That finished me off. I couldn't take it any more and started wailing. My third born child didn't show up to church that morning and didn't care about us or God. I had come to terms somewhat with my girls' beliefs, but now my SON? I had hoped that this last child would turn out differently than the girls. I thought maybe God would do something else with him. With my rage and disappointment about my oldest in my face, and now my son not being there, I felt pushed over the edge. Someone appeared next to me with white pants. It was a male but I didn't know who "JF". I latched onto him as he told me that God loved me over and over again. It was like someone had taken the lid off a huge love need and I kept blubbering and shaking, louder and louder. Then I looked up and saw it was one of my son's buds. I thought that it was very thoughtful of God to replace my son with someone else's son and I remember Jesus saying "woman, your son; son, your mother". Then "JF" said that when he came to church he worried about what people thought of him, that they judge him and he said that that is just spiritual pride and that he has to get rid of that evil in him. I had already admitted that I struggled with that before he finished the sentence and I felt so condemned. Right about that time I thought that it was inappropriate for me to be hanging on to a "strange" man like that. So, I straightened up, stopped crying and he got the point and left. I was fine.

One of the more scary times of healing for me concerned a male alter that I had split off called "POP". Pop didn't like the way I was being treated by men and so he became the alter that took over when male authority tried to force me into something I didn't want to do. I was so afraid to have a male alter; in fact, I couldn't even fathom such a thing. Of course his strength was gleaned from demons; he did not have that kind of power on his own. I knew he meant well and was trying to do the job he was given but he really caused some problems for me. I was hanging onto the control of my person as the alter POP wreaked havoc with my husband. God revealed to "DR" & "CR" that I had a male alter. This male alter was a member of the Knights of Columbus, a secret organization that Catholic men joined and he gained the demonic power that was involved with the organization. This alter was so powerful that the usual methods and prayers which worked on other alters did not work with this one. I had had an idea that I had a male alter 9 months previously but couldn't deal with that reality so I just pushed it out of my consciousness. It wasn't time for his healing yet.

And it didn't look like it was time for another alter who wound up conscious one Sunday morning. Finding herself in church with her oldest child who was giving her nothing but grief through her bad choices, she wound up with a protector up. I never did really worship or get anything much out of church and that upset me. I had this weird feeling; spacey, like I wasn't there, couldn't connect. Another of my parts, Needy, had been up recently and it might have been the oldest child's actions causing her to surface. If I had any doubt about someone else being up in church I didn't doubt it by the time I got home. I wanted to go out, to the movies, anywhere, or even better yet…EAT. The pressure was awful; I was very tired at the same time. I tried to just do what I had to do here but it was like trying to move bricks. The worst part was that I didn't know what was wrong. I finally said to my husband that something was wrong and when he listed the possible triggers, I had to admit it was that oldest child. I felt used, betrayed; I had betrayed myself, enabled her, etc. etc. And the pain I was feeling about my oldest grandchild and the yet unborn second female grandchild was high. I hate pain, I hate being out of control, I'm afraid and can't do anything about it so I EAT, and I feel better, or run away either in my mind or with my body; and I feel better. I didn't like it that God was not letting me use food and recreation to deny my pain anymore, but I know that it was best because the older I was getting the harder it was to lose the weight that I put on by binging. I couldn't believe the level of fear that I found when God opened me up. It was awful. But, as I talked about it with my husband and cried and shook it got less. I even was asking someone to help me but Jesus wasn't it. I didn't seem to know Him, didn't even think about asking Him to help until my husband said that I shouldn't be afraid. I felt stupid doing it, but I did. My husband told me the steps and I tried to do them but the unbelief remained. All I could see was me at 400 pounds and everyone laughing at me if I didn't control myself. THAT was where the panic was coming from. My husband prayed for me and I became ok. I never knew what was next in what I fondly called "life in the blender".

WAR INSIDE

I felt weird any time my husband went out of town. I was talking to Jesus and bible verse after bible verse after bible verse came through. Who was I? It reminded me of 4 years ago before I first went to that church how I used to hear a bible verse and it would comfort me, how I would remember a verse I had memorized or read and it would comfort me, not like now. Where have I been? Will I go there again? Am I here to stay? Will my husband be the same tomorrow? Who is he and where did he come from? It frightened me to think that I was someone else these last years or that I was someone else 4 years ago. I was so out of control, never knowing what would happen or if anything was real. I wished that whatever was blocking me from feeling Jesus right then would go away because I needed His love. I had prayer team duty on Sunday which made it 3 services that I had missed attending to take my turn at prayer. I told myself that Jesus wasn't limited to services at church to help me. He could do it in the car, at the retreat, at women's bible study, or anywhere else He pleases, I just missed feeling connected.

So the next Sunday we didn't make Sunday school because my husband had to go to work and our third child had to ride with us. That was just fine with me. Church was kind of empty and that made me feel weird. I did my usual; give hugs, say hello etc. Worship started and I went through the motions but could hear the internal war loud and clear which was unusual. WHAT ARE YOU DOING HERE? YOU DON'T WANT TO BE HERE!! I said YES, I DO and I understood that all you inside parts don't want to be here, that you thought it was a waste of time, but please, could you make a concession for those of us who did find meaning in this and allow us to do what we needed to do? I asked Jesus to calm them down so that I could worship. It got quiet but I was locked out emotionally, unable to connect again. I kept doing what I knew was right; feeling manipulated by, of all things, the music. It was like the worship team, God, or whoever, knew that the song they were playing jerked my emotional strings and so all they had done was play it, play it, play it and when I opened up emotionally then, zap – rage, condemnation, WAR inside. I didn't realize just how tired I was of all of this. I just felt nothing. Then I quit. No more singing, trying to do what was right, I QUIT. It wasn't very long before God "showed" me that He understood the struggle I went through. All of a sudden I had this revelation that God loved me even though I didn't like Him, His plan, His method, His timing and even though I had a WAR going on inside me that I was losing, which caused me much pain, shame, humiliation to acknowledge because I wanted to love Him more. He deserved more than the garbage I gave Him all the time and yet garbage was all I had to give. HE TOOK IT and still loved me. That revelation brought the tears and pain to the surface. I kept calling out to Jesus, telling Him how much I needed Him, how much I missed Him, how I couldn't live without Him every minute, would He please come and hold me? I'm too little to do this, please hide me from the bad guys who keep torturing me. They follow me everywhere, I have no peace, no rest, I have WAR and I was too little to fight a war. I could feel the crushing weight of the struggle that I went through day after day as my body had declared war against me and God with manifestations such as Gastro Esophageal Reflux Disease (GERD) and Fibromyalgia. I felt ground down to nothing again, a useless lump of nothing, at which time I remembered that we have this treasure in clay pots to show that this all surpassing power is from God and not from us. (2 Cor 4:7)

I never did get close to Jesus that day. I saw Him on His throne in heaven and then poof, nothing; but I did get relief for a few minutes. When prayer time was over, I was in tears again so I grabbed hold of my third child's hand and held onto him and then my husband came and he prayed for me in tongues and it was over. I was fine. I remember thanking God that this man wasn't tired of me, didn't put me down for being a weakling, a whiner, which he prayed for all the time without getting tired – Galatians 6:9 -

Let us not become weary in doing good for at the proper time we will reap a harvest if we do not give up. Isaiah 40:31 -Those that hope in the Lord will renew their strength, they will soar with wings like eagles, they will run and not grow weary, they will walk and not be faint.

As you can see from above there was a lot going on in my mind all the time. I had to figure out what I was hearing as being demons or alters; particularly the child alters who didn't understand any of this adult stuff. I had to deal with alters who didn't personally know Jesus and didn't want to hear about Him, as well as the protectors who would not let me see parts that were hurting, it was their job to keep those parts safe even if it meant keeping me from seeing them inside me and getting them to Jesus.

It was my usual day to see "DR" & "CR" and I had the most amazing healing by God that day. I am still humbled and awestruck by it and am uncomfortable about the way it happened; but I chose to believe it was for the good. At this particular meeting my husband was present. It was to be marriage counseling. It was only the second time in all the time I had been seeing "DR" & "CR" that we had had marriage counseling. They began by talking about helping us learn how to manage conflict without World War III type tactics. I almost immediately attacked them for suggesting that I might be doing anything wrong but they were taping this meeting and I knew it could be used against me over and over again in the future. I still wound up saying that I couldn't live with that lunatic. "DR" commented that he understood what

I meant because he got a glimpse of my husband's rage on the previous Monday at their appointment. He said that he had all he could do to stay in the room with that type of rage and he figured that I would be in the next county if he let that kind of anger go anywhere near me. My husband said he wasn't angry and hadn't had THAT type of anger since months ago when he pounded on the top of his car and screamed because SOMEONE had the nerve to LOCK his car and he couldn't get in it when he wanted to.

"CR" asked me how I felt about them being there with us and I said that I felt like I was in an inquisition with all of them against me. Notice the defensiveness and belief system of paranoia, like I couldn't get a fair hearing and would escape with only my skin and have to live with his rage the rest of my life because they didn't believe me.

"CR" asked my husband when was the last time that he was angry with me and let his emotions show. He couldn't remember. Meantime, I was sitting there spending all my energy to be quiet and not interrupt. Finally she asked my husband to ask Jesus when the last time was that he was angry with me and let his emotions show and he couldn't hear from Him. He rationalized instead. "CR" pointed out his rationalization and he became angry and fearful. She asked him why he was afraid and if he really wanted our marriage to work. He said yes but said that he didn't know why he was fearful. "CR" asked me if I remember the last time he was angry with me. I was finally given my time to vent and vent I did. I told them in explicit detail the events of the sex fiasco we had; feeling totally confident that they would see what I was talking about with him. They didn't. Instead it got turned around to be my fault. Actually "DR" was stating that since we seem to have great difficulty agreeing about sex that we needed some kind of compromise that my husband wouldn't be rejected and frustrated and I wouldn't be afraid, judged or used.

I sat there hearing that one of my inside parts wanted to cut him to shreds, but nothing was voiced. I was in control. Then the topic of headship came up when I began to talk about my husband's denial and power plays with me. "DR" asked me to tell him the last time that my husband pulled a power play and I couldn't other than at the campground. I didn't realize why I couldn't tell him and I got really angry because it looked like I was making things up and they were going to take his side. So, instead, I gave them a different scenario. "DR" said that I was wrong there too. No matter how I explained it, he didn't budge. And this really frustrated me because this was supposed to be an example of where he admitted he was wrong and asked me to forgive him instead of blame shifting, rationalization, and denial. "DR" said that as the head of the house I should have asked my husband's permission before doing what I did. When pressed about why my husband didn't just tell me no when I called him and told him that I had called and had a 7 pm appointment, my husband said that he was afraid to tell me no. "DR" said that my husband was emotionally afraid of me. "DR" also said that if I really had a problem with headship that we needed to talk about it. I said I didn't have a problem, but BOY DID I. At that point I couldn't take it anymore and just sat there. "DR" asked me something and I said WHATEVER YOU WANT, in clipped syllables. At that point "CR" asked me if I had any expectations about the session. I told her no, just to get out with my skin and she asked me how my skin was. I guess I had had enough at this point and I just said to her that this was all a 2 hour waste of her and "DR"'s time because when I left there I was never going to speak another word to my husband as long as I live because no matter what I did, I was wrong. If I mouthed off I was wrong, if I "submitted" I got told that Jesus didn't want me to be abused and that allowing my husband to abuse me was idolatry. I came there not even thinking we needed marriage counseling because things had been better since my husband got more healing the previous Monday and now I was stuck with having to submit to him and ask his permission before I did anything? No way. I said to "CR" that I thought that she was my friend, it turned out that she was my enemy. At that point I guess God finally broke through and revealed that someone else inside me was raging and I was ignoring her and denying she was there because I CAN'T still hate my husband for what he did fifteen years ago and lied about until last February (adultery). I had to be the "good" Christian woman and wife and that didn't include hating men and hating him.

This alter was up on vacation previously and caused the whole fiasco. I didn't want to admit it because it would make me look bad. I couldn't continue to hate him once I was challenged with a choice of letting Jesus heal me or going on the way I was. I knew it, so I wouldn't admit to being that way. Also, I had a major case of rejection and abandonment because I was still that hateful.

All of a sudden God showed me the truth about all of it and I started wailing. I got red in the face and buried my head in my husband's lap. I wanted to disappear. With that I said I was sorry to both of them for what came out of my mouth earlier and noted that I was a BITCH. "CR" asked Jesus who she was speaking to and I heard loud and clear: OVERWHELMED. She was a core part of me. She was the one who had so many religious demons and legalism issues. She also, evidently, had headship, submission and hate issues for men. She was the one who struggled with the Lordship issue 9 months earlier. I hadn't heard from her much at all since then (at least I didn't know it was her). Once Jesus told "CR" who she was speaking to, she had me ask Jesus if I was a bitch. He said no, I was just hurting and all the pain came shooting up. I was wracking and sobbing, feeling like I wanted to die. (I had experienced the wanting to die thing again on the third day of vacation after the sex fiasco, so I know it was her). "CR" had me try to see Jesus and I did. "CR" suggested that I get closer to Him and I was afraid. I got closer but He looked like a hologram, I got up closer still and finally jumped on His lap and cried and cried and cried. He said that He came just for people like me. I told Him how sorry I was and asked Him to take the pain. He did. I cried for a while though as I realized more and more what I had said and how I had acted. "CR" put her hand on my head and prayed in tongues for a while and I was able to calm down and hear Jesus. He said that it was time for Overwhelmed to come in from the cold (to use an expression). He meant to be integrated. I was shocked!!! I hadn't had an integration in ages and I didn't want one because I didn't believe that just because my parts have been to Jesus that they are all new and won't cause me trouble once integrated. But Jesus knew this and I had been so miserable with continuous demonic attack that I would do ANYTHING to stop that.

Some of the most painful emotional suffering was allowed by God to get me to the place that I would finally surrender and see things He needed me to see but wouldn't willingly do so. Add enough pressure and a new willingness was born. Many of my most powerful healings have come after that type of pressure on me.

I kept hearing "the whole counsel of God" as the reason she needed to be integrated and I hadn't quite understood what He'd meant. "CR" had me ask Jesus to get rid of the demons that had been tormenting me so terribly and I didn't think He would. In my mind I saw Him plunge a dynamite plunger and a huge explosion took place and they were gone. Then I saw hot oil pouring down on me and covering me. Then He gently pushed Overwhelmed backwards into the big person who was just standing there watching and "bloop" in she went. I felt odd, but good. Once she was inside me, she wouldn't be left alone as a target for Satan to pick on. That was where the whole counsel of God came in. I have all the necessary parts; mind, intellect, knowledge, and agreement with scriptures about life. I can hear and see Jesus and have the power of the Holy Spirit, all of which will work to make things easier for me and she wouldn't be a lone cannon anymore. I was astounded when it was over. I opened my eyes and looked around to see if it really happened. "DR" and "CR" and my husband were still there and no one was yelling or anything. I had been uncomfortable that my husband and "DR" were there to see my humiliation but my husband had seen my parts many times and had to live with them so it really wasn't anything new to him. What was new was her healing and integration. I was uncomfortable because of the brazenness and straightforwardness of Overwhelmed but they said that Jesus created that feistiness and He will use it for His good now that she was integrated. She was so street like with her talk about sex and other things. I couldn't talk like that without being terribly uncomfortable and embarrassed, but she just told it like it was. The good thing was that "CR" and "DR" didn't use street terms, they converted them to something kinder and gentler, but the understanding of what we were talking about was there and it was as if we were talking about the weather. No shock, gasp or amazement on their part. I still had a terrible time talking about sex, still felt it was dirty and so I was not to talk about it, no less do it. I knew I needed more healing. And yet I could be surprised by God still, as another episode of sex revealed.

IT WAS HOLY BECAUSE GOD CREATED IT

We had finally been able to go to bed one day after another knock down, drag out fight with our adult children. It wasn't exactly what I would recommend to set the mood for love!!!! And yet God had me remember what had happened previously when time stopped, there was world peace, and nothing mattered anymore. I could hear an inside part saying that physical intimacy was God's plan for a woman to be with her husband, it was HOLY because GOD created it. The more I thought of that and the fact that I was living my life in submission to God's will, the better it got. Then, once again, the panic and fear set in. I told my husband to promise he would NEVER, NEVER, NEVER do this with another woman; NEVER, NEVER, NEVER even LOOK at another woman because this was all I had to give him. I had let him into that sacred place inside me where there are NO secrets and in the past that wasn't good enough and he strayed. I didn't want him to ever stray again if this wasn't good enough or if my future behavior didn't stack up. He promised he wouldn't unless I died (and then I wouldn't care) and he prayed until I was able to get calm again. This had happened almost every time I was able to have that deep emotional release and abandon in the physical act. I was truly satisfied deep, deep inside me and all was well in the earth.

The next morning I went to church expectant, hoping to be able to feel God's presence and love. My second child was there and sat directly in front of me which made me nervous. I didn't want to have to watch her; I wanted to be able to concentrate on worship. She complained about how close the row was to the front of her and I told her that I use the aisle when that happens so I have enough room. That was the last thing I said to her that morning. I didn't see her worship, I didn't know why, but I didn't. The first song came on and I thought they had cranked the air way too low, but I then realized it was a constant flow of anointing to the point that I started to buckle because I gave in to it instead of fighting it. I sensed that God wanted to lay me out and I had a little internal discussion and told the demons that whatever God wanted or didn't was what I WANTED. The second song started and I sang the first section and my stomach started doing flip flops or something and then suddenly there was an explosion on me and I hit the floor doing what felt like 40 mph. My glasses flew off forward about 6 feet, I bounced. I sensed that someone had tried to catch me. I not only went down like a tornado had hit me, but the sound effects were hard to miss (because I sat second row center aisle) I started laughing, kicking and pounding my feet, shaking, etc. My face was flame red, I could feel it. There was so much power that I didn't realize what had happened until I was down. It was like I was in a dream, I sensed that I hit the floor, but felt nothing. I was concerned about my glasses breaking or getting stepped on, but I let go of that. I heard God say "like a mighty rushing wind" and I thought that a tornado would have been a more appropriate way of describing what had happened. I have never felt that amount of power in such a burst with so little warning (other than what I sensed was going to happen, but I never dreamed it would happen). Usually, it takes all of the worship songs, or almost all of them and it is a gradual filling to the point of struggling to stand up and finally letting go. NOT THIS TIME. Pow, Whoosh, Bang!!!! Glorious. I would shake and then stop and then another round of anointing would hit me and I would shake some more over and over until the end of worship. I tried to sit up and get up, but my body was like spaghetti, so I lay over on my stomach and stayed there until the end of the service. When I got up, I was concerned with what my middle child thought, but she smiled and approached me for lunch money, so I guess she was ok. I went up to be prayed for by the pastor and he asked God for another drink for me and then I realized I was already drunk in the Holy Spirit!!! At most bars they don't serve obviously drunk people, but God does. I felt such peace as the anointing made me into jelly again. I thought, this is too much, great physical intimacy and world peace yesterday and now this today!!! I'll take it. I've waited a long, long, long time and if God loves me this much (that was obvious), I'll take it. It was and is weird being Dissociative. I went into Wednesday night prayer and was fine. I got home and spent the next two hours ranting, raving, screaming, cursing, crying, etc, etc. etc. It was awful. And what I was doing all this about was some of what went on during prayer. "DM" was teaching out of the Song of Solomon and because of my negative belief system I thought he was doing a major job of guilting us into "dying to self". He said that the reason the apostles couldn't cast the demon out of that man was not because they didn't have faith, but because they were self centered. Jesus said: "How long will I put up with you…this kind comes out only by prayer and fasting". Mark 9: 29. "DM" said that the type of fasting that Jesus was talking about was not the eating type but the Isaiah 58 type: feed the poor, help the sick, etc and it was because they weren't doing THAT that God wouldn't answer their prayers and deliver that man. DM said that just like we wouldn't give our car keys to 3 year olds, that God won't give us his POWER until we have "grown up" and aren't baby Christians. Until we have CHARACTER. I sat there listening kind of disinterested in the whole thing. I felt God confirm to me that I was doing what was right and that what was happening to me **was** suffering (which was necessary if we wanted to share in God's glory) and I distinctly remember feeling like it was ok because I WAS A CHILD and children CAN'T BE grown ups. Other than that, I just wanted to leave. I didn't want to pray for anyone else. I remember looking at a male friend of mind and the tears came because I knew that he cared about me and wouldn't judge me. I looked at my other friend "SF" and felt compassion towards me. I even looked at father figure "FW" and thought that he cared about me. I didn't cry and I didn't leave. I kept praying that God would release me to leave without condemnation because I just didn't care. Prayer was very, very dry, very sterile, very religious (evidently an unsaved alter was up who thought that "good" Christians were phony by the sound of this). No one prayed anything of substance except "JM" who was the queen of "burning flesh" those days and maybe wanted a medal for it.

We had a stranger come in to bible study. He had been "driving by" and decided to check us out. The church people fussed over him, prayed for him. One of the women got him a glass of water because he kept coughing. I wanted to puke. Everybody trying to put on the "good Christian, caring brother" facade for this guy's benefit so they would look good and have the church look good. I couldn't sit by "TB" anymore because I felt such rage at her. I knew she looked down on me because of a reaction I had several weeks ago when we were together. She now knew she couldn't talk to me about her stuff because I go ballistic. Who really cared anyway? I didn't need her. She can go around pontificating about how WONDERFUL her life was, how WONDERFUL God was, how WONDERFUL our church was (the ladies in it). It didn't have to affect me. It was not nice to be that jealous and hateful of her and when

I'm not "up" the rest of me wasn't jealous, but it sure was surprising to see some one inside me was jealous.

You might say that I should have expected sex after that prayer meeting to be, shall we say, imperfect? I was so very angry from the meeting, and because I didn't want my husband to touch me. Sex is stupid, hurtful, ugly, dirty, disgusting. Feeling that way after the healing I had received earlier was crazy making. All of this must be make believe. Nothing really went on in my prayer ministry sessions. I came out exactly the way I went in. I didn't believe all this "little people" (alter) stuff. It was not possible to have other people inside of me who I have no control over. I AM IN CONTROL and I can choose to say @%$& everybody and just do what I have to do to survive. I didn't need God either. He didn't really know what was going on. As I typed this I felt sick. I'd typed out what demons are saying. WHY? I felt like an explosion was going to happen again when I got into church because the pressure was so strong that I felt like I would start screaming and never stop. It had been a while since I had been threatened with that type of Gestapo tactics by Satan. I actually thought I had it beat.

GESTAPO TACTICS

Speaking of Gestapo tactics, an event comes to mind of when my husband and I went to visit friends in Orlando over one Christmas. We were going through Universal Studio's City Walk, a long strip of restaurants with entertainment in most of them. We tried out one club after another and none of them were satisfying in any way. I started feeling sick and couldn't take being in that atmosphere so I signed to my husband to leave. It was very early, only 9 or 10 pm, but all of a sudden I had a bad taste in my mouth about this whole experience. As I started walking down the moving sidewalk I started to get pain in my jaw and I felt like I was being strangled or something. We got off the moving sidewalk and I had all I could do to ask my husband for help. I was going down fast. I couldn't even explain very well what I now know were demons choking me. Thankfully Jesus knew and had my husband run them off at the pass. I was feeling quite hopeless as I was being choked and when my husband tried to get them OUT of me. I informed him that I didn't know if they were

INSIDE, but demons they were, so he stopped trying to get them OUT of me and finally they released my throat. We then went to the movies and the last movie was horrific. I felt like I should have had the courage to get up and walk out, it was that bad; but as usual, the infighting was more than I wanted to deal with and so I stayed. I wasn't out of the theatre more than a minute when that same strangling feeling began again and while my husband did warfare I walked briskly to get out of that area of demonic activity for whatever reason they had grounds to be there. Once I was off the property, it was over. The rest of the vacation was much calmer and we enjoyed visiting with our friends.

Another time when I experienced "Gestapo tactics" was when my husband and I went to Walt Disney World. Our pastor had preached against going to WDW because it was bad for our kids. The whole premise of the place was bad. I pooh poohed him because I thought he was being ridiculous, and we went once more to WDW. This time we went to the new Animal Kingdom Park which had just opened. We went into the Lion King show and it had several thousand other children and adults with us in there. The show began and eventually progressed to their singing of the Lion King Theme Song: "Circle of Life". I immediately felt sick. My stomach felt like I was being stabbed. My head hurt, my eyes hurt, every joint, muscle, tendon, ligament and blood cell hurt. I began crying out to Jesus to help me and also told my husband to lay hands on me and pray. He did. What seemed like an eternity later (a few minutes in reality) I heard Jesus say that it was a spirit of deception that I was feeling and I was only feeling it because I had the gift of discerning of spirits. Jesus told me that all the other people would not recognize this spirit; they would just be deceived by this spirit to believe and teach to their children anti Christian beliefs. Yes, all that just from that song, thousands of people deceived. I guess my pastor was right, at least about the Animal Kingdom. I will never set foot in there again. Once Jesus told me what was going on we moved very quickly out of the arena and out of Animal Kingdom. Then the pain left for that day.

Wondering if I would ever learn, my husband and I went to Virginia Beach for vacation. While there we went to the IMAX theatre they had there. I cannot remember the titles of the films we had seen but they were not cinema type fare, they were educational, maybe about the ocean or something. We purchased our tickets and went inside to sit down. The movie began and very shortly thereafter I felt sick. My stomach felt like I was being stabbed. My head hurt, my eyes hurt, every joint, muscle, tendon, ligament and blood cell hurt. I began crying out to Jesus to help me as I ran out of that theatre and to our car in the parking garage. I told my husband to pray for me. He did. What seemed like an eternity later (a few minutes in reality), it eased up but was not gone. So, we left the parking garage in search of lunch. We had time before the next movie. I chalked it up to some type of demonic attack and that I was only feeling it because I had the gift of discerning of spirits. I wasn't sure anything was wrong with the movie we were watching. After lunch we returned for our second feature and sat down. It wasn't more than a few minutes into the movie when the pain began again double the intensity of the first attack. OK, I may be a little slow but I KNEW what this was and I grabbed my husband and dragged him out of the movie. We left and drove quite a distance before the pain subsided. It was not until we got home to our permanent residence that I found out that Va. Beach was the home of Edgar Cayce, the founder of Mind Control. No doubt that was where the attack was coming from. We had gone into Satan's territory or should I say the stronghold of Mind Control. I am thankful Jesus got us out of there and that the attacks subsided. I do not think that I will go to anymore IMAX movies no matter what the content is. Because in reality I had a previous experience with an IMAX film that I took my niece who was maybe 8 or 10 at the time to. It was about evolution even though they didn't bill it that way, they just named it something or other Indian something. It started out innocent enough but about 1/3 of the way in it started with Indian's ancestral spirits and other things they worshipped as God. Additionally, all the Indian women were topless in full view of the viewing patron. I had such a spirit of lust come over me that I became physically aroused and finally pleasured myself right in the theatre seat next to my niece. It was very dark and loud in there and there weren't any other people seated around us. I was very humiliated and shamed immediately thereafter but I learned a lesson about innocent sounding/looking movies and the spirits that they bring with them to cause people to sin. Jesus forgave me when I said I was sorry but that shame lasted until I received healing for that event.

WON'T SOMEONE HELP THE SMALL CHILD?

I was depressed many of the years that God was healing me even with medicine. One particular day I had finished dinner just as my husband came home from work. He asked me how I was and I didn't really want to burden him with still another day of my depression; but before I knew it, the Tsunami hit and I wailed and wailed and wailed for a good long period of time. It was the strangest thing because I could see a small child in an alley in the dark, all alone. I kept hearing "won't someone help the small child" and at the same time I could feel the fear, pain, abandonment, hopelessness, etc. that she was in. My husband started talking to me about Jesus and I knew I had heard about Him but that He was not available to me, other people who were worth it got Him. My husband continued to talk about Jesus and I got more and more agitated and upset. I told him there were 4 BILLION people out there for Jesus to take care of; He has no time for me and doesn't even KNOW

I EXIST. He continued to try to get me to see Jesus, but all I saw was black and the child in the alley. He kept praying and at one point I told him that I felt like he was pushing me and he apologized and said he was just trying to help. I thanked him for that but told him that for some reason it wasn't time for whomever she was to get healed and set free. He said fine.

Evidently it was this child alter who brought forth the following dream: I was in my Auntie's house and for some reason was cleaning her bathroom. I began with the toilet. It overflowed and I never noticed until there was 3 inches of water on the floor. I saw that and attempted to stop it but it only stopped for as long as I held the ball up inside the toilet tank. The water on the floor went down the toilet somehow and I thought I was ok but suddenly it started overflowing again. At that point, I opened the door and yelled for help from my Auntie and she came in. She wasn't in a rage with me; she helped me get it right which was very unusual.

I know that dream sounded innocent enough but it was frightening. I was in a situation where I had tried everything I knew to do it right and yet it exploded in a mess. That feeling of surprised helplessness was awful. It reminded me of other dreams that I kept having where I am totally out of control and awful things happen because of it and then I get blamed, punished, ridiculed, abandoned, etc. etc. and I was still feeling that way when it was bedtime the next night. I was begging Jesus that night to just let me be, just finish this where it was, stop the torture, but I knew that I had to go through to the end and that whatever Jesus was doing, it was for my good. I was so very weary of these explosions everyday. I couldn't get relief for more than a few hours and I found myself very angry about that even though I didn't want to be.

For the first several years of the healing process I had a part time job to pay my way through college to complete my Bachelor's Degree. As the time marched forward, the healing became more difficult and it finally came to the point where I could no longer work. I needed time after the counseling sessions to rest because my brain was mush and I lived in a fog mentally. I was in constant pain physically; there was no relief from the pressure. There came the day where I had to tell my boss that I couldn't work anymore and so I called her. She didn't want to hear it. She offered me more money, guilted me to try to get me to stay. I had not wanted to tell her I was sick and that that was why I couldn't work. I figured it would go against me for future employment. I had spoken to her on a Wednesday and we had bible study that night at church. As usual they offered prayer ministry to whoever needed it and it took all the courage I could muster to get in that chair. Once in the chair I had the impossible task of trying to tell them what was wrong without telling them because I was embarrassed/humiliated to find myself in that situation, feeling like I was basically having a nervous breakdown. I didn't do a very good job but somehow the necessary information came out of me and almost everyone in the entire room gathered around me and tried to touch some part of me to pray. Father figure FW prayed and declared that I was loved by him and everyone else. I had never heard anyone say that except my best friend, wife of my doctor, so I was blown away. Another woman who I liked started praying and basically said that she wasn't spiritually mature enough to even pray for me!!!!!!! ME??????? My eyes were closed but I could tell who was praying by the voice. Suddenly a woman took hold of my head and started praying in tongues loudly and with much passion. To me it sounded like a lullaby. The only other person who sounded like that and had that effect on me up to that day was "CR" and I knew it wasn't her because they had already moved away. As she prayed I got so much anointing that I basically fell out of the chair sideways and lay on the floor. It was after everyone but my best friend and her husband and my husband and I had left that I told them that I was DID. She was very accepting and just asked a few questions so that she would know how to recognize when someone else was up and how she should act to whoever was up when we were together. And she has been faithful with loving all of me and loving whoever was up when we were together.

There was a tremendous display of God's power on me that night. The next day I called my boss and told her I was sick and could not work and that I would call her when I was feeling better. I have not returned to work there and I have peace about it. God is taking care of our finances.

For a period of time my husband and I and sometimes other people from church would go to a church

2+ hours away from us where they had an all night prayer/praise meeting every Friday night. One of the nights that we went was very sparsely attended and the leaders of the service didn't even arrive until after 9 pm (worship started at 7 pm). There were several words of knowledge and prophetic words and some of them could apply to me so when the call was given, I went up with one of the other women who came with us that night for prayer. The minister was working his way down the line of people who came up and when he got to me I felt like he was trying to push me down which wasn't so bad except that the "catcher" was trying to keep me up. The result was that I felt like I was being broken in half. I wound up on the floor but felt nothing. The one thing that struck me was that there was no reverence there that I could see. I am not one that believes that unless you wind up on the floor that you haven't been to church but when I am down and feel nothing it bothers me and even more so, my alters. On the way home I was very angry because it felt like a waste of time having traveled that far and I never felt God's presence. My body started to hurt, shooting pains down my legs and I was very restless like I was stuck in the car with nothing to do all the way home. I remember turning sideways toward the car door and looking out at the highway lights as we went by. Several of the others in the car were sound asleep and I was mad that I couldn't sleep because of the pain and restlessness. I then chose to go to a place in my brain where I could escape it all. Where no one could get to me, where I didn't have to answer to anyone or be hurt by anyone. This was the third time recently that I had done that and I realized that I hadn't journaled it. The first time I did it I was thinking about High School and how we read the book "The Glass Menagerie" and I now understood how that girl felt and how it was much better to live in a world that she created where no one can hurt her than to live in the hostile world we lived in now. The second time I did this I can't remember what the circumstances were but I recall remembering the movie "Nell" in which they find a young woman who was raised by a deaf person who died and this girl had no speech. When she got frightened, she went into a routine that the psychiatrist in the movie said was a "calming" type of self preservation. I felt like this was what I was doing. What was really weird about the ride home from that church was that choosing to do that was the last thing I remembered until my husband was making such a racket while driving that he woke me up. The pains in my legs seemed to have stopped and I was instantly asleep once I chose to go to that place in my mind. The problem is that that place was somewhere Jesus wasn't. I saw Him as part of the hostile environment I had to live in. I didn't think that was good, but really didn't understand it all, so I just recorded what happened and let it go.

By the time Sunday morning came I couldn't wake up. We missed Sunday school which was good because after I read something in the bulletin when we finally arrived, I was dealing with a 4 alarm rage again. I tried to push down the rage that was triggered but a woman got up to sing and it triggered a memory of my father driving down the highway from the Big City with my (then alive) grandfather in the car. I got hysterical. No matter how much I called out to Jesus to help me it continued completely through worship and all of the pastoral prayer. It got so bad that I was stomping my left foot in rage at having to find myself in this position again. The humiliation was awful. A teenage friend of my middle child moved closer and patted me on the back and I had to hold myself back from pushing her away. I had just been daring God to send someone over to me so I could deck them. This was another "life in the exploding volcano" experience for me. I had no control. Suddenly I realized that I WAS going to walk out and never come back, that it was finally going to happen and the terror that that realization caused was awful. I had sat down and pulled my coat over me to muffle the sound of my wracking cry. My face was all red again. Someone needed to get out of the aisle that I was blocking and I was ignoring them peck on my back because I thought they wanted to talk to me or pray for me. Finally I sat up and let the poor person through. She was sorry she had to bother me. I stopped loudly wracking sometime during the sermon, but things would pop up and the tears would come again and again. My husband was sitting up in the sound booth and he came over and sat down. I was feeling hopeless and suicidal again when my husband prayed for me (without speaking out loud) and it was finally over. Another alter had surfaced as described above. I didn't realize that was what had happened until later, but her issues were conditional love based only on performance, works righteousness, TRUST NO ONE (they are all liars). She also was interested in committing suicide just to punish everyone; the ultimate act of control. You cannot torture me anymore because I am dead. You cannot make me stay here and be tortured forever. That whole thing scared me. I'd been suicidal before because of pain, but never because of cold, calculated, rebellion. Knowing that I would go to heaven anyway leaves no real reason NOT to do it. I was tired of having to force myself to drag through each day with no meaning, no fulfillment, and no peace. My life was being wasted day by day because I had been disabled to the point of not being able to function and if I did function, it didn't make any difference because no one cares. Nothing brought me satisfaction or a feeling that my existence meant anything. If I were dead no one would care for very long, I would be easily forgotten.

It wasn't until the next counseling session that God told me that the alter above's name was Rage. Of course, Rage would fit the description of what I have been experiencing. Somehow I thought that she had been healed already. Rage had a right to the feelings she had, having been "underground" for most of the last several years in all that pain.

After the above incident, Rage was up again as I was reading about Codependency. I had read 75 pages of the book about Codependency and God showed me some things. He showed me that my rage reaction against Him was wrong because I was not doing what I needed to be doing for myself and I can't blame Him for that. That codependency stuff set me free. I felt free. When I don't do everything to gain approval and love from people, even if it is bad for me, I am free. I can do what I want and not feel guilty. I do not have to take care of everyone else in the whole world. They can and must take care of themselves. I realized that that was what went on with me in church. I was so worried about my friends/people that I have this invisible doom/pressure on me that I wasn't even aware it was there. I think that Rage was talking to me about how much she didn't like my husband and that I wasn't being honest with my husband and telling him so. I told her that I understood her situation and she quieted down. It was scary to hear that inside me. Another revelation was the fact that in dysfunctional homes, no matter how much a child tried to please or not make mistakes, it was never enough and there was never forgiveness because that was the power that parents used to control and manipulate the child. The child will continue to strive to please and be used by the parent if they were not told they were forgiven. That security was missing and the child was terrified so they kept trying and trying and trying to please. When I read that it rang such a bell. NO WONDER I can never feel forgiven, why I don't believe people forgive. I can't believe I was reliving my childhood, but it appeared I was. Somewhere in that reading God hit me with a bolt of lightning in my stomach. It was like at that very first small group meeting years ago, but not as severe. At that meeting I felt like the chair I was sitting in was going to go backwards at 100 mph and go right through the wall with me in it, the power was so great. This time, there was much less power, but the type of anointing was definitely the same type and I felt it. It surprised me. What a wonderful way God chose to show He loved me. I think He also did something else because I felt better emotionally. I spent the day doing what I wanted instead of what I thought everyone else would want me to do. I could hear the voices inside telling me that I couldn't/ shouldn't/mustn't do this or that and I simply told them no. I don't have to. I think Miss Hypervigilance was up because she was always reporting to me the sensory things that were going on. She was particularly active when it came to anything that might even remotely lead to sex. When she did that, I felt fear and closed down. Net result; I lost out. I was glad God was giving me this revelation even though it hurt. It was the pathway to healing.

That evening we were watching ER on the TV (one of my favorites). Two of the main characters (Lucy & Carter) were treating a man who they thought was off mentally so they called for a Psych consult. Carter left the room to get something and when he came back the man was gone and Lucy was down on the floor, evidently the victim of a stabbing (she dies before the end of the show). As Carter was checking her out, the man appeared from behind the door and stabbed Carter too. He passed out before being able to call for help.

The next thing I knew I had lost it. That sick, black, eeriness came over me or up in me or something. I was completely out of control. I cried out to Jesus to save me because I was paralyzed emotionally and intellectually. Trapped, helpless. I felt like a small child who couldn't even think a rational thought. The world closed in on me quickly. The hopelessness and despair were overwhelming. I was trying to push them down, rationalize them away somehow. I felt like I was living in the Twilight Zone. This was such a shock to me that it was like that time warp you get into in labor where your body is so far ahead of your mind that it causes much confusion. I had a lot of difficulty even expressing a rational thought to my husband. I just kept asking Jesus to protect me, to rescue me, to run my life for me because I couldn't run it myself. Then....it was over. Whatever alter in me was triggered was gone. To where I didn't know but my husband suspected it was a wee one and I agreed with him. He said that he felt pain watching that show also. He prayed and prayed for me and I finally fell asleep.

Church came around again in only 3 days and I felt a little apprehensive going in. That mushroomed into full discomfort and a strong desire to leave. I couldn't connect in worship at all. I started talking to myself about it being ok, trying to convince myself of that fact. It didn't work. I had to sit down because my legs were hurting so bad to stand and I could hear the "works righteousness" tirade by someone inside me telling me what kind of a miserable Christian I was because I couldn't connect and couldn't stand up. I felt embarrassed, but upon hearing the tirade told myself the truth, that it wasn't my behavior but my heart that matters. The only problem was that my heart was dead. I didn't want to be there. My husband saw me and asked me why I didn't ask him for help and I said I didn't know. He prayed, but I got no relief. I cried a little and just resolved to accept my situation. I had flashbacks of the previous visit to that church 2+ hours away where I was trapped for hours in so much physical pain and disorientation which didn't help. That just increased my desire to leave. Prayer time in the service was spent by my looking around the sanctuary wondering why people thought all this praying was necessary as if someone hears them. Or cares? Another round of condemnation began when I realized what I was thinking and just how awful it was. God WILL punish me for being so hateful and callous and refusing to believe in Him and that scared me. I told my husband that I was going to leave. He said fine. I told him I had a book in the car I could read until they were done. As soon as I said it I was afraid again. The fear came from realizing that I WOULD just walk out and never come back because I thought church was a waste. It was not relevant to the real world. People do just fine without all this religiousness, in fact they are happier because they are constantly tormented by the SHOULDS; by the rules and regulations of church. Outside church they can be real and their friends don't judge them because they know they are just as bad as them. They actually have FUN instead of always being told to pray more, give up more, fast more and be told that whatever they were doing wasn't enough!!! That same fear that I felt months ago which was in the nature of a volcano returned right then, but not in that much fury. I asked Jesus to save me from myself, to not let me do what I wanted to do – walk out and never come back. I didn't know what was worse, the fear of leaving or the fear of staying to have to listen to the abortion women who were to give their testimony that morning. They didn't realize how much the doctors helped women who were trapped by men's irresponsible behavior with no one to help them once it was too late. That was what you got when you needed love – pregnant and abandoned. When you went to the "church" for help, they wouldn't help you; neither would your father or the father of the child. The only ones who would help you were the doctors' who didn't judge you and relieved you of your problem. I didn't see why a woman had to pay the price all the time while men run free. Even if she carried the baby and delivered the child, she was marked as bad, while the man (whoever he was) was not thought bad. Why women are punished for trusting a man who said he cared and would be there and then wasn't. SEX was dangerous and should be avoided at all costs, and men were dangerous liars who used women and should also be avoided at all costs. NEVER believe them because if you do you will wind up in a mess.

I had run into those abortion women in the children's room before service and my alter Blunt decided to dump all our secrets to them. She was fine about it, but I was angry she did it. She always does these things without thinking about me, her name illustrates her nature.

Service was finally starting and I was able to feel some anointing in the room, but I also felt the walls it hit emotionally. I was not happy and had to spend more time telling myself it was ok while listening to someone inside wailing about being locked out, being excluded, desperately wanting something she was not getting. I also heard someone saying that church is church, it was not an emotional trip, that was the past and now it was time to get real and accept that church was church, you go there, hear the sermon, go out and do good deeds and come back again next week and do it all over again.

It sounds like Rage was up again there and at the next service she was again. She was angry because church was so weird. There is no set pattern, people just do anything and they are all too close physically. Pastors get up there and tell everyone it is the time of Jubilee, JUST DO IT. JUST release yourself, JUST forgive, JUST….IF I **COULD JUST DO IT**, it would be great, but I couldn't. I think they drum this stuff up just to hype everyone emotionally, to try to get them into action. All that hoopla at Friday night service and look how few people even CAME to church Sunday. If all this stuff they were selling us were true, our PEOPLE would be there at service like they were 4 or 5 years ago. Then the pastor goes and puts pressure on a poor woman by singling her out in the congregation and telling her that she had a "song" for the church body. I felt the panic in me go off just thinking about what if he tries to do that to me. What I do is PERSONAL, between ME and GOD alone. That type of INVASION was unacceptable. Of course, the beautiful song I heard coming from her ceased when the pastor put that microphone near her. Then, when church was over, it was time for more whooping and hollering, trying to hype everyone up again, even though no one knew what they were doing up there. I just wanted OUT, but once again, my husband was so busy doing his thing that I was stuck, so I went up for prayer. It was like dragging a dead person up there. I told the pastor I went to for prayer that God had told me that I had Him locked in prison inside me, so I set Him free and apologized for doing that. I also felt like the word a brother had about my being afraid of entering in was true. I didn't realize it until he said it that I was afraid. But he said that Jesus wanted to take my hand and go with me because it looked like a big Chasm and indeed it felt like it to me. The pastor and my husband, and my friend and her husband, and our mutual male friend, started praying for me but Rage decided we weren't going anywhere. These people were NOT going to manipulate her and get her to fall over and then terrible things can happen that she had no control over. NO WAY. It was very hard for me who wanted something to have her so set against all this, but I stood there and let them pray figuring if God wanted to He could do something with Rage. The pastor then prayed something about anyone inside me at "any age" that needed whatever, I can't remember. I remember thinking that Jesus was gentle and loving and that I could trust Him. I went down and I guess the same people prayed more for me but I felt nothing. Afterward we went to my friend and her husband's house and played cards. I also drank a couple of wine coolers and so did she and I remembered how wonderful it was to get wasted, no one to bother me, nothing to think about, just floating. We laughed and laughed as we played. We went home and I felt miserable realizing what a wasted night it was drinking and being just short of obscene with the language and the remarks made. I was ashamed at what little desire I had to do what was right. It was as if my conscience had died. I had that same feeling that people only liked me because I looked good, did good things; and acted like a martyr, played out again. People WILL NOT like me if I don't perform, come to church, believe the same things as them, do what I'm told in counseling; and RAGE does NOT want to cooperate with this and I'm miserable.

I FELT CRAZY AGAIN

In the morning I was crying because I felt crazy again. THIS IS NOT REAL; THIS IS NOT HAPPENING TO ME, SO WHAT IS MY PROBLEM??? People think that they have the right to invade my brain and I think I have to let them. Sick. Church is a private thing. You go there, it is quiet, people keep their distance, mind their business, do things decently and in order every time and the only time you have to deal with the priests is in confession unless you do something stupid like talk while he's talking or fall asleep or laugh or misbehave bad enough in school, THEN you are in big trouble.

My husband said that maybe there wasn't a Rage, maybe this wasn't DID. I told him he was right. The pastor said it was over; it was the time of Jubilee. I've had prophecy after prophecy, after prophecy that the time for my restoration was soon and then NOW. So, if that is the case, then I'm well. Or, the best I will ever be. WOW that was encouraging, NOT. I felt like this whole thing had been one great big mistake, except for the fact that after 2+ years with "DR" every week and with "CR" sometimes that I was still all messed up. My husband said that Jesus would take care of me and then prayed for me. I was having big theological questions, like, will God really do what He said, and will He heal me completely? Does He still love me with all this miserable attitude and continuous rebellion? WAS He really in control, did He even know what was going on and if He did, did He care? I believed there was a God up there somewhere, but He has nothing to do with everyday life. Jesus was up there at His right hand doing something sometimes for someone who really needs it, but for the rest of us?????? He told us what to do and now we needed to JUST DO IT. Hopefully we will have done enough that He'll like us in the end. I then sat down and read Charles Stanley's devotional reading about barriers to Faith and trusting in God. He said to place your trust in the omnipotent potential of an all-knowing God who loves you completely and will never allow you to experience shame or disgrace. I guess I was involved with some other god because I felt plenty ashamed and disgraced because of my behavior. I can't even say I love Him with my whole heart. All this for no reason either.

Even though the above was incorrect, for that alter at that time, it was true. There were many reasons I behaved and believed that way, all related to the abusive and neglectful childhood I experienced. Sometimes I wondered if I would EVER function what I perceived from others was NORMAL because it seemed that as soon as one alter had her say there were many waiting their turn for healing. God was

SO very gracious to me despite my continued poor behavior, unbelief, believing in lies instead of His truth. This process went on for 5 years during which time I lost both parents, all 3 children rebelled, a male grandchild died (and another male one died 3 years later), my brain refused to function properly resulting in crushing depression, anxiety that needed medication to get relief from, our home being burglarized to the tune of $5,000 stolen, my husband confessing two counts of adultery. A year later I broke my ankle on church property and was in a cast for 15 weeks (very painful because I broke it in 5 places and had reconstructive surgery) and a wheelchair/walker to get around; and when it was removed I felt like a pirate because my ankle was so stiff that I had to take a step with the good leg and then hoist the no longer broken one up next to it.

We went to a conference a month later during which Bill Johnson prayed for my ankle and my ankle was healed instantly and was as normal as the other one, **Praise God**.

After those years passed, God saw fit to send us more than 50 people over two years to minister to and we saw mighty miracles of healing and deliverance in those people's lives. And then there was a women's retreat one fall and as the group leader I wound up in the middle of three very envious women all trying to control one of their adult daughters (27 years old) that wound up in my small group. It led to a screaming match during which I was called a liar (the pastor's wife ran the meeting) and I was asked not to try to defend myself against those lies. So I sat quietly the entire time and every time there was a meeting concerning what happened.

I almost had a breakdown and spent 4 years suffering the effects of that event, some of which I mentioned earlier in the book. God did more healing and deliverance in the areas of trusting anyone and believing I was worth anything anymore. We went for training in generational deliverance and God did my healing there!!

The "powers that be" basically shut down our ministry in their church 4 years previously by preaching against us from the pulpit (as "so and so", not using our names) and within a year we were seeing no one. I had requested to be a leader of a women's small group 3 years after the incident described above and I was told No, not even with my husband co-leading. What used to be thanks from the pastor and his wife for ministering to their son became NO you can't have a small group, no deliverance referrals, and no appointments for healing.

There was also the brouhaha about DID. Those in power in the church above had believed in it 4 years earlier but now that the counseling pastor and his wife had left they decided no one ever had DID, those who thought they did were simply naïve and easy to manipulate into thinking they did have DID. Eventually I had to take a stand for what I KNEW was true for me; that there was such a thing as DID and I had it and had had it for my whole life. I left the church but my husband didn't. I sought counseling from a counselor that Tom Hawkin's ministry recommended and only after that counselor told us that he could not see it working out at that church did my husband come to church with me where we now attend. But by then the damage was done. I had tried to get help within the church we left by the head of the prayer ministry there but upon meeting with us for several hours he said he could not be of any help to us. I had put a lot of confidence in him and was astounded and hurt when he said he couldn't help us. I felt that my husband had not told the truth during that meeting and I kept telling them that he was not being truthful; maybe that was why the prayer minister said he couldn't help us. I left that meeting feeling totally helpless and hopeless. I was trying to stay with my husband because we had had prophecy that we would have a ministry **together**. If we split up, there would be no ministry for me; for him perhaps still because he didn't cause the problem at the women's retreat. I finally had to take my stand and if we had no ministry, oh well. I was so miserable that I would do anything to have peace, even giving up working with the wounded. I was so terrified of making the wrong choice, taking a stand that others didn't agree with. I was afraid of being labeled "crazy" because of my stand on the issue of DID. I thought my husband was in complete denial again and I was ready to have my oldest child help me draft a statement of "separate maintenance" where my husband would be forced to live elsewhere while I stayed in our house when God did something and the next day my husband was acting like who he was before the whole women's retreat debacle. It had to be God because he went from vicious towards me to tolerable. I forgot to mention that during the year that I begged him to choose me instead of the old church that he had blood clots in his lungs which should have killed him, ripped up his knee which will require a replacement in time, and went blind in one eye (in that order). I also had back surgery suddenly and quickly (right before he went blind in one eye) for a blown out disc that was causing me to not be able to use my one leg properly. I was down for 6 full weeks, restricted from sitting for more than 20 minutes at a time, so my choices were standing or lying most of the time.

After he went blind he decided that maybe he was missing something that God was trying to tell him which was good; but he had rage when he found out his lack of sight was permanent and was caused by an erectile dysfunction medicine which he took in combination with his anti-blood clotting medicine. Now he had no sight in one eye and no more sex ever. It was fine with me because I didn't ever want to have sex with him again, and thanks to hormones and psychiatric drugs couldn't feel anything or have any kind of release, and my sex drive disappeared completely also. My husband believes that having sex was what took away his eyesight so he isn't very interested in trying even if he COULD have an erection. While my husband didn't blame me verbally for his condition, I was the closest one to him and so I suffered as he tried to work on the anger and resentment he felt but was denying he had any feelings like that. My doctor suggested seeing a urologist to get another way to restore sex and my husband was not interested (hence the conclusion that he thinks it is SEX not the drugs he took to help his ED that caused his blindness in one eye and he doesn't want to go completely blind so no more sex).

Periodically I would still try to get off the medications that interfered with sex and ability to respond/feel anything and very quickly the symptoms that caused me to need medications appeared again so I had to go back on them. I tried switching medications for the same reason and once again very quickly the symptoms returned. I believe that God can heal me but so far I still need the medications to function normally.

Determined not to give in to the devil and his evil we enrolled in three training courses about DID and Generational Deliverance that year. The following year we attended an intern level week of training on Generational Deliverance and successfully completed it. We are now able to receive referrals from the founder of the organization we are certified in. But before we even became certified, God had sent a family who needed help our way and we were trying to help them get free using the training we received.

I don't know if you noticed as you were reading but once it was determined by my counselors that I had DID there was a fundamental shift in the way my counseling was carried out. Previous to the DID designation I would go to "DR" for memory healing and then separately go to "DR", "CR", "CF", "AMK" etc. for only deliverance.

Once it was determined that I had DID I went to "CR" & "CF" and in each session whichever parts of me wanted to talk and/or receive healing and deliverance were given their turn. "CR" & "CF" had been trained by Tom Hawkins how to address both the alters' healing issues and bring deliverance to each alter in a much faster, more efficient way since there were so many parts of me. This discovery explains somewhat why there were so many failed deliverance appointments and why the very issues that were healed by healing of the memories one week would return all over again as if nothing had ever been done only weeks later. The part in which the demons reside and the memory is stored needed to be brought to Jesus for healing individually.

An example of this type of healing is as follows: I had been in a hospital with a girlfriend whose daughter was having a double mastectomy at the same age as my oldest child when I broke a 32 oz cup of soda I had brought her directly on top of her brand new computer. It immediately shut down and despite vigorous effort by her and her husband, it would not work. I had a major reaction when her husband asked me to please leave after I did that. This reaction was the strongest one I had felt like it since the last healing of the memories/deliverance when "DR" & "CR" & "CF" were still ministering to me. I had been relaying this story to our new counselor who was trained by Tom Hawkins when suddenly I found myself confused. I was feeling accusation and condemnation and I tried to fight back with the truth of God. The counselor, "CG" began asking me questions about where I was and what was going on. Turns out I was back in grade school feeling that people could see through me and see how stupid I really was. "CG" asked me if this was the first time I had felt this way and I began to feel humiliated, my face was red and I began crying. It appeared I was back in 3rd grade where that nun slapped me in the face in front of the whole class. It was discovered that I wasn't stupid then or now because my inner world was one of chaos and therefore I couldn't concentrate, understand, and retain, etc. what was being taught. I was shipped from relative to relative while my mother was in the nut hut (hee, hee, hee) and my father was like an IED (Improvised Explosive Device), I never knew when he was going to go off. Next "CG" asked me to look for Jesus, that He was there. I saw Him and I went over and sat on His lap and snuggled my head into His chest. I told him about the spilled soda and the whole story. The humiliation was unbearable, I just wanted to disappear. Being 53 and still that stupid was more than I could take. Previously I could "disappear" but what really brought it home was that there was NO escape as a child. No where to hide, both physically and emotionally. I NEVER had any privacy, was never allowed a thought of my own, and was continuously humiliated by the sisters and family members. I was so very tired that I kept yawning and yawning and yawning (demons can exit a person through yawns, they can exit any way that uses air, pneumo, as they are spirits) and crying on and on. CG told me to give all the pain to Jesus. Jesus said I was NOT bad, stupid, needy, and selfish; and the list goes on and on. Jesus said that needing love was ok, my parents were supposed to have given me love but they didn't have it to give so I looked for it "elsewhere". Jesus put Plexiglas between me and those evil ugly thugs (demons) that were throwing mud filled balloons at me. HA!!!! They didn't get me!! Jesus pointed His index finger at them and told them to GO and they slinked off. While Jesus was holding me, these black scales (I called them shingles) were falling off me revealing a clean girl. Then the spirit of fear thought that he could carry on and Jesus drop kicked him!!!!!! I was laughing. It was so hard to believe that He found me wherever it was that I was pushed off into with all that pain, amazing that He could love me that much. Then we danced, just me and Him. Almost like a little girl whose feet are standing on her daddy's while he swirled her around. Eventually Jesus was doing Hip Hop (although His gown made it difficult). I love Hip Hop dancing. Thinking I was done, I just rested there. But I wasn't done. "CR" brought up my first grandson's drowning and my 2nd grandson's asphyxiation and a torrent of pain came exploding up. I never got to tell my first grandson how much I loved him before he died so I did it then. Jesus showed me that my grandson didn't suffer, Jesus put a bubble around Himself and my grandson and took him to heaven with Him and he is with the truckload of relatives of mine already up there. My second grandson was in heaven with my nephew who also died as an infant as well. Jesus was personally taking care of them in heaven, He wasn't looking the other way when they died, and the devil didn't win. More demons were drop kicked; I was confessing the sin of believing the lies of the enemy that God wasn't really good after all. I had thought that I was beyond redeeming, way too bad to be loved, had used up all my allotment of healing, was crazy, a failure even at my best. But Jesus said no, no one was crazy, things just got messed up. Nothing I could have done would have changed it, I did what I could and it was good enough. In church that next Wednesday our pastor taught on James 1. When he finished he was praying when he said that God was telling him to tell the members of the class that God could heal people who didn't trust anyone anymore, who couldn't be vulnerable, especially with church authority. It hit me like a secret weapon and I broke into tears and went to the ladies' room to hide that I was crying. The following Sunday Pastor once again mentioned church authority and.................. NOTHING!! I was healed that Wednesday, Praise God.

THANKS

I hope my story has given you hope, freedom and a better understanding of just how much God the Father, Son and Holy Spirit love you and will bring you through to healing. NEVER give up; it WILL be done according to God's Plan.

If you want to ask me questions, please address them to the publisher of this book who will forward them to me, I am happy to help where I can.

CPSIA information can be obtained
at www.ICGtesting.com
Printed in the USA
LVHW09s1757100918
589686LV00001B/9/P